OTHER BOOKS BY VICTOR D. MARSHALL

A Journey of the Bold and the Young: Living on the Edge

Set the Captives Free: Experiencing Healing Through Holistic Restoration

Set the Captives Free: 12 Studies for Groups or Individuals

Pastoral 6
Perspectives & Issues

ON THE ROAD TO FORGIVENESS

Experiencing Healing on the Way

VICTOR D. MARSHALL

authorHOUSE®

AuthorHouse™ UK
1663 Liberty Drive
Bloomington, IN 47403 USA
www.authorhouse.co.uk
Phone: 0800.197.4150

Published by AuthorHouse 05/27/2015

ISBN: 978-1-5049-4298-0 (sc)
ISBN: 978-1-5049-4299-7 (e)

Print information available on the last page.

CONTENTS

DEDICATED TO

The various congregations, groups and individuals with whom my family and I have worked in presenting this material and other topics relating to emotional health. You motivated me to produce this volume since it is your desire to promote emotional wellness in your own life and in others.

ACKNOWLEDGEMENTS

FOREWORD

By
Grace Walsh

I have known and worked with Victor Marshall for several years and have witnessed his passion for promoting emotional health. His keen interest has been confirmed by this excellent book he has produced, entitled *On the Road to Forgiveness: Experiencing Healing on The Way,* as well as several other books which he has written on the subject. I am sure that some of you who are about to read his book may have developed anger or resentment in your heart at one point or another in your life. Someone may have hurt you or life may have disappointed you, an experience which you may not have recovered from up until now. I pray that this volume, *On the Road to Forgiveness,* will open your heart and make you see the urgent importance of living free from any kind of bitterness, resentment or un-forgiveness.

With the entire British nation, and even global societies, increasingly concerned about health, Victor Marshall has produced an excellent compilation on the topic of interpersonal forgiveness. The principles he has presented can mean the difference between life and death. He has put forward a handy guide that will offer many people life-saving options and also give them tools and sound principles that will be of benefit in various situations, especially when help from professionals is not available.

The author has taken a wholistic approach to forgiveness and its effects on health. In support of his position, several studies have linked un-forgiveness to a number of emotional, mental, physical and spiritual conditions associated with mortality and longevity. Therefore, it gives me great pleasure in recommending his book, *On the Road to Forgiveness: Experiencing Healing on The Way*, as a very useful source of practical information for those who, for any reason, are still grappling with issues of forgiveness. I am honoured to be given the opportunity to write comments on this masterpiece.

Unfortunately we cannot go through life and never get bruised, hurt or wounded. Human experience shows us that life is filled with injustices. However, Victor shows us from his book that we can be free from the pain of these wounds by letting go of the past painful issues, because the roots of un-forgiveness are insidious. They grow deep below the surface and take hold deep within us.

The book takes into account several new perspectives that have emerged recently and which seem to be gaining currency in emotional health. The approach considers the wholeness and integrity of the individual. Therefore, the work is quite comprehensive, reflecting the expanded scope of emotional health today.

It is my prayer that as you read this book, you will learn that when you process anger in a healthy manner and forgive the person who has hurt you, then you are doing yourself a favour.

Grace Walsh
BSc Nursing, BA Social Sciences, RMN,
Director for Health Ministries, Community Services and
Disabilities Co-ordinator
North England Conference of Seventh-day Adventists,
United Kingdom

FOREWORD

By
Dwight van Ommeren

You hold the fourth book on emotional health from the hand of my dear friend and colleague, Victor Marshall, whom I have known since 2004. With an in-depth knowledge on the topic of horizontal forgiveness, he takes the reader on an emotional, practical, social, spiritual and theological journey in search of answers. He also illustrates that forgiveness deals with our past, present and future relationships and that they impact on various core issues of humanity such as emotional wellness.

By asking questions, the writer seduces the reader to look at this topic in another thought-provoking way. In my opinion, no one else so far, other than Victor Marshall, has blended psychology, spirituality and theology to take the reader ably on such a journey of inspirational discoveries about interpersonal forgiveness. By introducing intriguing cases, he leads the reader right into the practical side of the matter, namely, what is *forgiveness* and how we can be healed by adopting a forgiving attitude. Moreover, he then proceeds with very good analytical discussions, from which you will notice immediately that he has done his research thoroughly. The results sometimes are unexpected, sometimes exciting and sometimes confronting.

When you read *On the Road to Forgiveness: Experiencing Healing on the Way,* it is very clear that having a faith is key to extending forgiveness, in that, it is the Divine One who inspires and equips us with the capacity to forgive others. Throughout this intriguing book you hold in your hands, Victor Marshall also reinforces the importance of spirituality, since without it we would not have a firm foundation on which to extend forgiveness. Victor Marshall expresses this view when he writes that "the moments of prayer provide comfort and relief; and create a calm and peaceful atmosphere in which individuals, who struggle with painful issues, can reflect on the power of Christ."

Are you struggling to forgive someone? Are you waiting to be forgiven? Do you assist individuals who are experiencing emotional, mental/ psychological or spiritual issues? This book would help individuals such as you to experience emotional freedom which leads to being healed. Furthermore, every chapter is enriched with an interesting principle such as:

To forgive, a person needs to experience some degree of healing, and to experience healing, an individual needs to forgive themselves and others.

When we hold onto our painful past experiences and memories, we lose opportunities for emotional and spiritual progress.

Reframing your difficult situation contributes to one's willingness to surrender the painful past situation.

Accepting responsibility for an adverse situation, desiring a change of heart and working towards a settled mind, assist with emotional progress.

At the end of every chapter the writer provides a summary. This makes the book a real joy to read seeing that it reviews the main points and helps you to understand the subject better. I recommend *On the Road to Forgiveness* as a must read, for it will help the reader to understand forgiveness in greater depth. The book also shows that it is essential to develop various qualities such as compassion and courage, seeing that the journey on the road to forgiveness can be challenging, painful and tough.

I am very proud of my good friend and colleague, I dearly appreciate his depth and insight in the subject, his scholarly knowledge and his great devotion to God.

Pastor Dwight van Ommeren
MA Theology (Pastoral Studies)
President of the South Netherlands District
of Seventh-day Adventists
Rotterdam, THE NETHERLANDS

PREFACE

"I will never forgive her," twenty-year old S blurted out.

It was a sunny summer afternoon while I was conducting a study with a few young people that this eye-opening, nerve-awakening and stunning declaration popped out from one of the students.

"So why don't you want to forgive her?" I probed.

"She hurt me," Stacy revealed aggressively, "and she doesn't deserve my forgiveness."

This statement propelled me to think hard and long. Later, I asked myself many questions: *Why doesn't she want to forgive the lady? What could she have done Stacy that was so terrible? Can she go on living without forgiving the person?* I was stunned because I could not find the answers.

Well it was while preparing for an old year's religious service that I was inspired to speak from the biblical book of Philippians. In the third chapter, as I reflected on verses seven to fourteen, the proverbial light bulb came on in my head. As I prepared the message, five stages of forgiveness popped out at me. One of them was healing. It was there that I saw the link between forgiveness and healing.

"That's it! Now I know why S couldn't forgive the lady. It's because her wounds were not healed. She was still hurting," I mused to myself.

Having received this valuable revelation, I proceeded to develop the first sermon entitled, *Leave the Past in the Past.* As I write this volume, I propose that there is mutual interdependence between forgiveness and healing. Out of this proposition, I have developed the driving principle on which this volume is based and which has also driven the perspectives held on the subject and the sub-topics.

Soon after, in 2009, my close friend and pastoral colleague in the Netherlands invited me to conduct a weekend prayer conference for one of his churches. No doubt, one of the presentations was on forgiveness. Since 2011, I have been conducting emotional health seminars and hosting various conferences on emotional wellness. More often than not, forgiveness features highly in these events.

In late 2013, I received a call from one of my ministerial colleagues in Manchester, United Kingdom, asking me to conduct a weekend programme on emotional health with two of his congregations. As we discussed the needs of the congregations, the topic of forgiveness was high on the agenda for both congregations. While preparing the presentations, an urge overpowered me to turn the presentation on forgiveness into a book. This must have been divine inspiration seeing that I completed three chapters in three weeks. However, on sharing the plan for my project with many of the attendees at those weekend programmes, they undoubtedly urged me to complete the book because they desperately wanted to have one.

S's stark revelation motivated me to focus on interpersonal/horizontal forgiveness, seeing that most people struggle deeply with this aspect of their life. However, while most books on the subject provide a physiological perspective, I have attempted to illustrate the psychological journey individuals undergo when they are faced with the issue of interpersonal forgiveness. My intentions for writing this volume is to examine some of the psychological approaches, issues, perspectives and processes relating to the journey of forgiveness., underpinned by spirituality and Adventist Health and theological perspectives.

Over the past sixteen months I spent exploring and researching this topic, I have had the chance to analyse relevant Biblical passages using bible dictionaries, bible commentaries, exegetical tools, and critically reading the work of recent and past scholars. Out of this process, I have discovered a number of significant insights. One such insight is that un-surrendered painful past difficulties create a psychological and spiritual impact. Additionally, I unearthed the view that leaving the painful past issues in the past involves three processes. Additionally, my research has revealed that forgiving others contributes to the fulfilment of our psychological needs. These were some of the personal discoveries that forced me to revise and expand the content of my initial seminars and sermons on forgiveness.

To ensure that you, the reader, find it easy to interact with the material in this volume, each chapter has been sub-divided under appropriate headings. A brief summary is provided at the end of each chapter. Furthermore, to help you assimilate and grasp a greater understanding of the topics, a reflective study guide has been prepared and placed in Appendix A.

May you experience a life-changing journey as you turn the pages of this new book!

Victor D. Marshall

Sheffield, United Kingdom

May Day, 2015

INTRODUCTION

Presidential Pardon! Royal Pardon! Political Pardon! Ecclesiastical Pardon! These are familiar and popular phrases used in political and religious circles over the years. Such debatable acts have been extended by Presidents such as Abraham Lincoln; and Roman Catholic Pontiffs among other world leaders. History is replete with individuals who experienced mercy: R. M. Nixon and C. W. Weinberger are among those on a long list. The perpetrator may have engaged in immoral wrongs. Each wrong-doer could be punished in one form or another, with punishments range from doing hours of community work to life imprisonment. Instead, there is a change of heart and the wrong-doer receives a second chance.

Victims who experience a change of heart after suffering from such heinous crimes undoubtedly would have gone on an emotional and possibly spiritual journey. While on this journey, victims would have been experiencing guilt and pain among other emotions. In moving along such a journey, the injured individuals would need to gather emotional strength in order to reach this point in their life. Importantly, during this time, such individuals would need to display compassion and extend mercy. How is this possible? It all comes down to one word-forgiveness.

Travelling on the road to forgiveness is emotionally draining, especially if the wounds are deep and wide. So the major proposal in this volume is that, hurting individuals, in carrying unresolved past painful issues, experience difficulties with interpersonal/horizontal forgiveness and therefore, are unable to progress emotionally and spiritually. Furthermore, if the issue has been left unresolved for a protracted period of time, the willingness to engage in forgiveness can be suspended. Nevertheless, for hurting victims to experience healing on the way, it is vital that they work continuously and in an enduring manner, at extending forgiveness.

I pause at this time to ponder on a few searching questions: What is the meaning of forgiveness? How is it played out among individuals? What impact does extending forgiveness have on us? It is such questions and more which *On the Road to Forgiveness: Experiencing Healing on the Way* seeks to address. Nevertheless, in beginning the process of shedding light on the meaning of forgiveness, let us examine the definition in the third edition of *The Oxford Dictionary and Thesaurus*. It defines the verb 'to forgive' as: "1: cease to feel angry or resentful towards; pardon an offender or offence. 2. Remit or let off a debt." Based on this definition, a person who extends forgiveness engages in the act of putting aside bitterness, deep-seated hatred, and extending grace and mercy to one who should have suffered the consequences. Nevertheless, seeing that this definition provides a generic view, it would be useful to examine a few definitions which focus on specific elements of forgiveness.

Gary Collins shares the view that "forgiveness can be very difficult, especially in situations that are unjust. … We need help in giving up feelings of revenge, in casting off all feelings of hatred, …."[1] No wonder Everett L. Worthington Jr. defines forgiveness as "an altruistic act, an act of doing a nice thing that the other person does not deserve, helping the other person have the gift of gratitude. Forgiveness is where justice and mercy come together." [2] Having considered these views, the question on how the act of forgiveness is played out leads me to propose the following definition in this volume:

Forgiveness is a journey which involves facing, surrendering and turning away from one's past painful situation in an effort to experience progressively, some degree of emotional and spiritual healing in order to move forward purposefully.

My proposed definition consists of five stages which creates the journey that helps us in developing the capacity to extend forgiveness to others and be forgiven as seen in Fig 0.1 below. In going through the five stages, seen in the diagram below, the journey, anchored in intercessory prayer, can equip us with emotional strength, thereby enabling us to forgive others.

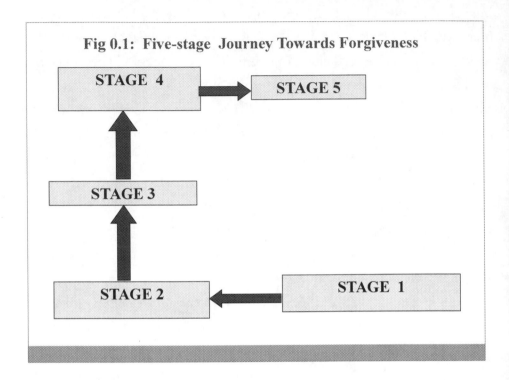

I also propose that individuals move through these imaginary stages, inwardly, as they seek to extend and experience forgiveness. During the processes, individuals would need to be intentional about wanting to progress. Applying the principles taught in this volume and engaging in therapeutic work can assist individuals in progressing along the journey and by extension, contribute immensely to their healing. Furthermore, this volume addresses the topic of forgiveness which is the first journey in the deliverance phase, the second of four such phases shown in Fig. 0.2 in the hierarchy of holistic restoration programme below.[3] The need to devote an entire book to interpersonal forgiveness is based on my view that it is a necessary process to be taken in order that we be delivered from the debilitating emotional and spiritual issues we face so often.

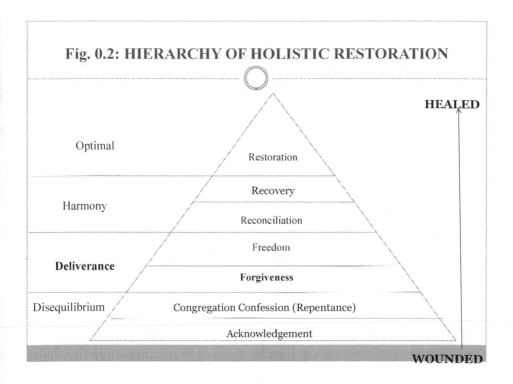

Fig. 0.2: HIERARCHY OF HOLISTIC RESTORATION

In exploring the question of what is forgiveness, it is essential to be aware that forgiveness occurs on three dimensions (1) intra-personal; (2) interpersonal/horizontal; and (3) divine/vertical. However, in this volume, I will focus on interpersonal forgiveness because it features prominently in the Christological instructions: "If you forgive those who sin against you, your heavenly Father will forgive you. But if you refuse to forgive others, your Father will not forgive your sins" (Mt 6:14-15, NLT). Additionally, this focus is adopted because it is at this level that many people struggle, thus prolonging the rate at which they experience personal healing for past painful hurts and wounds.

On the Road to Forgiveness seeks to assist young and middle-aged adults who are or have been wounded emotionally, physically, psychologically or spiritually. Such individuals experience a raging battle in the mind which tends to be engulfed with infinite questions: How can I ever forgive that person who took away a major part of my life? Why did my progress have to pause for so long? What will happen to the wrongdoer? Should I have to take the first step on this journey? What would happen if I refuse to extend forgiveness? This volume has been written to assist you in understanding that interpersonal forgiveness is an essential journey which hurting individuals must undergo in order to progress emotionally and spiritually.

I also need to offer a disclaimer in introducing this book. A major feature of this volume is the case studies entitled "Thinking Analytically". These hypothetical cases have been included for the sole purpose of illustrating a point. However, it is recognised that because we live in a broken world, some of these stories could be the experiences of tens of thousands of hurting individuals worldwide. I do not in any way seek to minimize or belittle hurting people's experiences, but simply to identify general situations with which we suffer and from which we can experience healing.

In this volume, interpersonal or horizontal forgiveness, used interchangeably, is the focal theme which emerges consistently. Each of us at some point in our life will be attacked, hurt, offended or misunderstood. Others may experience abuse or have been abused (be it emotional, physical, psychological, sexual or spiritual). How do we deal with the concept of forgiveness? Do we forgive the perpetrator? Do we live with our open wounds indefinitely? Such questions serve to stir us into thinking profoundly about the subject of interpersonal forgiveness, knowing that it is linked closely to one's emotional wellbeing. Furthermore, when you peruse the upcoming pages of this volume, you will also encounter sub-themes such as courage, dysfunctionality, emotional freedom, power of the mind and restoration.

Unlike most volumes on the subject of forgiveness, *On the Road to Forgiveness* is unique, in that it presents, from biblical and academic perspectives, a five-stage journey necessary for individuals to begin to heal. In particular, it portrays the interdependence between horizontal forgiveness and personal healing, and argues that:

To forgive, a person needs to experience some degree of healing, and to experience healing, an individual needs to forgive themselves and others.[4]

In our fast-paced society, where some individuals seem void of empathy, it is vital to understand the concept of interpersonal forgiveness. Importantly, hurting individuals, counselling clients, Christian counsellors, guidance counsellors, psychologists, psychotherapists and other providers of pastoral care will encounter appropriate material in this volume to aid them in providing therapeutic care. I am aware that individuals from different backgrounds, professions and schools of theology and psychology could interact with the material contained in *On the Road to Forgiveness*. However, the views shared in this volume portray a Christian perspective of forgiveness within the context of emotional and spiritual healing at the individual and congregational levels.

Furthermore, in presenting a psycho-spiritual perspective of horizontal forgiveness, I have attempted an integrative approach in bringing together psychology, spirituality and theology to bear on the issue of forgiveness or the lack of this psychological construct. Thus, the chapters reflect a theology from Adventist tradition, an Adventist health perspective, a broad perspective of spirituality from evangelical Christianity and a broader input of psychology. In particular, I have provided exegetical analyses of various biblical texts in order to present a richer understanding of the biblical data being used. And so, the aim is to apply these three areas to the concept of forgiveness.

In order to ensure that the teaching in this volume is anchored soundly, a number of subsequent principles have been identified. Thus, each chapter in this book is founded upon the philosophical principles as seen hereafter.

EIGHT PRINCIPLES OF INTERPERSONAL/
HORIZONTAL FORGIVENESS

On engaging in horizontal forgiveness, you experience progress when you…

1. Intentionally face the painful past situation and agree to address it.
2. Refuse to hold onto painful past experiences and memories which prevent you from experiencing emotional and spiritual progress.
3. Reframe your difficult situation which contributes to one's willingness to surrender the painful past situation.
4. Accept responsibility for an adverse situation, desire a change of heart and work towards a settled mind.
5. Emotionally let go of the past painful issues, discern the hindrances to your progress, discover and pursue a Christ-directed goal.
6. Recognise that to forgive, you need to experience some degree of healing, and to experience healing, you need to forgive yourself and others.
7. Experience emotional and spiritual healing which creates a desire in you to move on.
8. Strive for the ultimate goal which requires you to focus on issues of eternal value.

The book is not intended to be purely academic nor technical, thus I anticipate that your interaction with the volume will be easy, engaging and smooth. May your journey *On the Road to Forgiveness* either lead you to experience salvation through Christ, the Redeemer, or be prepared for His Second Coming, as you seek to experience healing on the way!

1

FACING THE PAINFUL MOMENT

"Pastor, would it not have been better to leave those issues alone?" she inquired firmly with her eyes wide open.

"What are you thinking?" I purposefully and tactfully asked.

"There is no need to bring up those painful memories. It's too painful," she continued.

These were the terse emphatic sentiments Jean shared in relation to the year-long healing programme, entitled *A Journey towards Total Wholeness.* It was some four or five months before writing this book that the leadership team and I took one of my congregations through the programme. We had reached the stage when we were focusing on the topic of reconciliation during the month. In the presentation during the worship service, I strategically and cautiously focused on three sub-themes of identity, safety and belonging.

I had been conveying the message that we must be willing to face the painful issue by acknowledging or admitting that a problem exists. Admitting the situation enables us to become aware of the debilitating, destructive, draining issue in our life. Such an attitude prevents us from adopting the psychological defence mechanism of denial. At this moment, a number of questions could flood our mind: Why should we have to face our monstrous demons? How beneficial is facing our painful past situations? Wouldn't it be easier for us to 'let sleeping dogs lie?' Jean continued to share her sentiments with me during the luncheon recess.

"What do you think would happen if we didn't address the issues?" I pushed.

"Nothing," she replied confidently, "we would just continue as we are at present."

"I firmly believe that if we do not address the issues they will come back to haunt us," I counselled.

"Well, I still don't see it."

After I convincingly explained to her the need to engage in the healing programme and the need to address the destructive issues which were lurking in the dark crevices of the congregation, she quietly surrendered to this perspective and then turned away.

PROMOTING EMOTIONAL WELLBEING

In a similar light, individuals have baggage and painful background issues lurking in their life and tend to carry them into various spheres of life. At times, the absence of resources to promote our emotional wellbeing results in a 'cohobblopot' of painful behaviours, deadly thoughts and destructive attitudes. We find ourselves bringing past painful issues onto the job, into the church, into our marriage or into the lecture room. Often times, they are covert and hidden in the heart. No doubt, we are aware and cognizant that we have unresolved issues lurking in the misty recesses of our heart. Such issues, be it an extra-marital affair, a false accusation or a stolen idea, if not forgiven and resolved, can hinder our healing and progress in various aspects of our lives.

So what resources are appropriate for developing our emotional wellbeing? I suggest two types of resources which seem appropriate: spiritual and psychological. First, in relation to the spiritual resources, individuals with a Christian worldview bring to bear intercessory prayer as an important spiritual discipline onto their painful issues.

> **Unresolved painful past issues can contribute to low productivity, and a dysfunctional personhood in different spheres of one's life.**

The ...... responsibility lies with the individual and the corporate body of believers who seek to develop a relationship with the Infinite One, through 'communing' with Him.[5] Moreover, when religious individuals approach the

3

God of Heaven, He responds according to His purpose, thus indicating that prayer is a dialogue and therefore, consists of a 'listening' phase. Such an act enables the individual to experience divine aid in times of difficulties.

It is noted that unresolved issues bring pain which can be difficult to bear. However, we can gain comfort from the Psalmist David's example when he called out to God in prayer:

> "O God, listen to my cry!
>   Hear my prayer!
> From the ends of the earth,
>   I cry to you for help
>   when my heart is overwhelmed.
> Lead me to the towering rock of safety,
>   for you are my safe refuge,
>   a fortress where my enemies cannot reach me.
> Let me live forever in your sanctuary,
>   safe beneath the shelter of your wings!"
> _____ (Psalm 61:1-3, NIV).

David presents his appeal to the God of Heaven, using language that suggests he was troubled. Clauses such as "O God, listen to my cry!" and "I cry to you for help" and " when my heart is overwhelmed" suggest that he was disturbed inwardly. Here David appeals to God's auditory ability, thereby longing for Him to respond to the pleas of his desperate heart. Nevertheless, like David, when we are troubled, we can turn to the God of Heaven who is able to impart divine grace, and emotional strength, and help us develop appropriate spiritual virtues to aid with emotional progress.

Furthermore, individuals who engage in intercessory prayer, receive support and encouragement through their faith in the Divine One. It is this active and fervent belief which provides the spiritual energy with which they engage in prayer continuously, while experiencing spiritual growth.[6] Additionally, intercessory prayer assists in providing healing for our emotional and spiritual wounds.[7] Ultimately, during our various ordeals, we must acknowledge that prayer is an integral element of spiritual and psychological health. Additionally, prayer is central to our spirituality, in that it helps us to approach the God of Heaven with our cares and concerns.[8] On engaging in intercessory prayer, individuals must maintain faith in God, out of which joy emerges, thus signifying progress in relation to adverse situations.

Apart from the personal advantages, intercessory prayer changes one's atmosphere. It provides an environment conducive to victory and living the Christian life.[9] Ellen G. White, in commenting on the significance of prayer, concludes that "prayer is the opening of the heart to God as to a friend. Not that it is necessary in order to make known to God what we are, but in order to enable us to receive Him. Prayer does not bring God down to us, but brings us up to Him."[10] The moments of prayer provide comfort and relief; and create a calm and peaceful atmosphere in which individuals, who struggle with painful issues, can reflect on the power of Christ.

Another spiritual resource is the Holy Scriptures. Studying the Word of God aids us in putting our circumstances in perspective. In applying the many principles captured in the Holy Word, we can acquire insightful and valuable counsel. A central role of the Scriptures exists in the following verse: "Your word is a lamp for my feet, a light on my path" (Psalm 119:105, NIV). The implication is that studying the Holy Scriptures provides guidance for our life and ensures that, on following the instructions, our journey through life will be illuminated.

The Christological admission in John 6:63, noting that "the Spirit gives life; the flesh counts for nothing. The words I have spoken to you – they are full of the Spirit and life" (NIV), reveals the potential power in the Word of God to bring hope to a troubled individual. On studying the Sacred

Scriptures, it is another avenue whereby hurting individuals can acquire inner strength and be helped to develop their faith in the Compassionate Christ who cares about their injuries and is eager to heal their gaping wounds.

When we think about the varying sentiments hurting people express about themselves and others, we would agree that reflecting on or meditating on the Word of God can help individuals reframe their thoughts about their situation. Those who are troubled by a perpetrator can be assured of Christ's comforting power as portrayed in this joyful psalm:

"On my bed I remember you;
   I think of you through the watches of the night.
⁷ Because you are my help,
   I sing in the shadow of your wings.
⁸ I cling to you;
   your right hand upholds me."

_____ (Psalm 63:6-8, NIV).

In essence, the studying of the Holy Scriptures is beneficial in that "the mind may go deeper and still deeper in its research, gathering strength with every effort to comprehend truth; and yet there is an infinity beyond."[11] Reflecting, meditating on and praying through the Scriptures contribute to our emotional and spiritual journey on *the road to forgiveness*. The benefits are valuable since "the Bible presents a boundless field for the imagination, as much higher and more ennobling in character than the superficial creations of the unsanctified intellect as the heavens are higher than the earth."[12]

BOX 1.1: THINKING ANALYTICALLY
D and J, his brother, have had problems over the amount of their inheritance after their parents died. J, the younger became very angry and openly expressed his hatred for D. "I wished you were with mum and dad now," J constantly yelled. In spite of D's attempt to discuss the matter, J, as he is affectionately called, hurt by the measly thousand pounds he received, ignores D's phone calls. As time elapsed, J cut all communication with his brother. Whenever, he attends his local place of worship, he would ignore D's wife, and the children. To add fuel to the fire, the nephews, nieces and cousins are very fond of D and often speak highly of him.

Another spiritual resource which could contribute to promoting emotional wellbeing is theological reflection. Robert L. Kinast advises that "theological reflection is a method to help people learn from their own experience and involves experience, reflection and action, whereby it tries to help a person (or group) discover God's presence in that person's (or group's) experience."[13] From this perspective, people are guided in making meaningful interpretations of their experiences and are led to encounter the divine presence in their life as it is seen even at the present time.

Fritz Guy contends that "theological thinking … facilitates growth because the more we know about, and understand the meaning of such spiritual realities as the activity of God, intercessory prayer, Sabbath … the more profoundly we can experience these realities.[14] Since this spiritual resource seeks to assist individuals in grasping "a responsive and transforming knowledge of the character and activity of God",[15] it is hoped that individuals who seek to encounter God would internalise the meaning of human existence.

In light of the above thoughts on theological reflection, how do we integrate our beliefs, faith and values into a broken, damaged or wounded life? Since this spiritual activity is most effective in small groups, the implication is that those who are burdened, hurting, or wounded, travel best *on the road to forgiveness* while being in the presence of others. That is, the support and resources from pastoral caregivers are integral to the emotional and spiritual progress of this category of people. Put another way, the wounded who desire healing, advance quicker emotionally in the context of pastoral visitations. This form of pastoral care draws on pastoral counselling, reflection on the Holy Scriptures and on intercessory prayer among other spiritual disciplines, thereby providing the emotional and spiritual foundation needed to engage in horizontal forgiveness.

Christian counselling and psychotherapy are two psychological resources that can be tapped into in promoting emotional wellbeing. Counselling practitioners deal with "developmental issues, addressing and resolving specific problems, making decisions, coping with crisis, developing personal insight and knowledge, working through feelings of inner conflict or improving relationships with others."[16] On the other hand, when we mention psychotherapy, we refer to "the informed and intentional application of clinical methods and interpersonal stances derived from established psychological principles for the purpose of assisting people to modify their behaviors [sic], cognitions, emotions, and/or other personal characteristics in directions that the participants deem desirable."[17] These resources seek to uncover in a deeper way, the effects residing in the unconscious mind, thereby healing the mind using psychological methods.

The need for such resources arises because of the inability to address issues, possibly because of fear. Such a negative emotion leads to three reactions: fight, flight or freeze. In this case, individuals who are unwilling to address issues could be on the run emotionally, physically, psychologically or spiritually. However, to avoid the negative impact from being on the run, individuals may employ repression as a defence mechanism. Psychologists note that the most popular defence mechanism is "repression, an act of pushing a fact, a feeling, a thought or memory into the unconscious mind."[18] This defence mechanism impacts negatively on the defender, to the extent that the person also represses everything which is related to the targeted individual in order to avoid the issue resurfacing. Consequently, a cyclic response emerges, whereby all other associated parties, directly and indirectly related, are ostracised.

For example, in the above-mentioned battle between D and J, the negative attitude extends to everyone in D's circle of influence. Clearly D is unwilling to forgive or incapable of forgiving his brother because of repressed anger which could be transformed into bitterness. Such behaviour and attitude expend a large amount of psychological energy, which a wounded individual is unable to sustain, especially if the pain has been prolonged. Even though this mechanism saves hurting unforgiving individuals from pain, using it for too long with the same situation could be dangerous. Individuals who lack appropriate emotional resources and who may be unable to employ other defence mechanisms such as denial, projection or rationalisation tend to become depressed and could become psychiatrically ill. In light of the above perspectives, hurting individuals are encouraged to take the journey *on the road to forgiveness* which consists of five stages.

FIVE-STAGE JOURNEY

The perspectives shared above lead to the following question: How do I develop the emotional capacity to address my painful past situation? The response to such a question lies in the principle below:

To face your painful past situation intentionally and agree to address it, provides individuals with the first step towards healing.

The first stage of this journey is facing your painful past. Engaging in this process

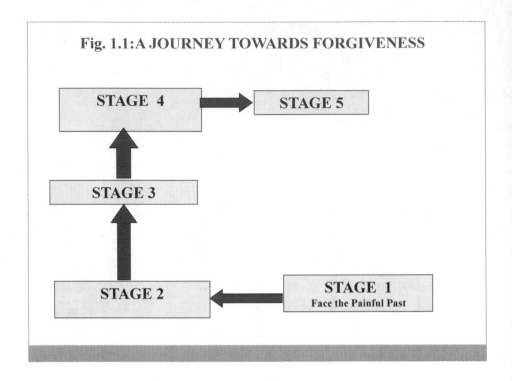

Fig. 1.1: A JOURNEY TOWARDS FORGIVENESS

requires inner honesty, openness and being vulnerable with ourselves. In providing biblical data through which the above-mentioned major question can be addressed, we turn to Philippians 3:3-6. In this text, Paul, the biblical writer of these verses, shares some personal and insightful details about his background with the Christian believers at Philippi, an ancient Macedonian city. Scripture gives us a glimpse of his autobiographical data: "though I could have confidence in my own effort if anyone could. Indeed, if others have reason for confidence in their own efforts, I have even more! I was circumcised when I was eight days old. I am a pure-blooded citizen of Israel and a member of the tribe of Benjamin—a real Hebrew if there ever was one! I was a member of the Pharisees, who demand the strictest obedience to the Jewish law. I was so zealous that I harshly persecuted the church. And as for righteousness, I obeyed the law without fault" (Phil 3:4-6, NLT). I wondered what inspired the biblical writer to stir up his past life. What benefits would it have on his original audience, and by extension, on his contemporary readers?

Just as how the Apostle Paul faced painful situations, past difficult memories, and adverse experiences, we also need to confront and deal with those situations which have the potential to impede our progress emotionally and spiritually. It is noticeable that Paul bravely catalogued his previous antagonistic behaviour on two occasions (Acts 22:4-5; 26:9-11).

BOX 1.2: PAUL'S PAST ATTITUDES, BEHAVIOURS AND EXPERIENCES	
Pre-Conversion Life	**Post-Conversion Life**
Paul, as a strict Pharisee • Supervised the stoning of Stephen • Persecuted Christians • Harassed members of the Early Church • Imprisoned Christians • Enforced blasphemous behaviour • Intensely hated members of the Early Church	Paul, as a Christian and Apostle was • Stoned for preaching about Jesus • Robbed & Shipwrecked • Experienced sleeplessness, hunger, thirst • Imprisoned for preaching the Gospel • Mistreated by strangers and fellow-countrymen

We are reminded that Paul, "being a man of decided mind and strong purpose, he became very bitter in his opposition to Christianity, after having once entirely settled in his mind that the views of the priests and scribes were right. His zeal led him to voluntarily engage in persecuting the believers. He caused holy men to be dragged before the councils, and to be imprisoned or condemned to death without evidence of any offense, save their faith in Jesus."[19] Moreover, John T. Squires asserts that the identification of Paul's background was for "apologetic purposes, not in order to provide autobiographical information."[20] This suggests that individuals need to recognise the emotional and psychological damage which their undesirable actions have caused and seek for ways to eliminate the negative effects.

In order to confront a difficult situation or a person who has injured you, it also required humility and maturity. Engaging in horizontal forgiveness

I pause to consider the following questions: What could have driven Paul to such extremes? How would displaying such pre-conversion attitudes have benefited him? Individuals who refrain from engaging in horizontal forgiveness or avoid addressing painful situations seem to be motivated by the need for power (n Pow). By not releasing the wounded individual, unrepentant perpetrators hold the unmistaken view that they are in control of the situation and the victim, and that they have the power to decide when to apologise.

BOX 1.3: THINKING ANALYTICALLY

J shared with her counsellor that she was having difficulties with D, a member of her religious community. J further related that D, a highly paid married individual, has been casting unkind looks at her, put her down whenever she spoke to her and always interjected and 'cried down' her views. Jan confronted D about her treatment. But D emphatically retorted that she was not ready to deal with the impasse between them. In the meantime, J was hurting and on the verge of attending another place of worship until she had the emotional capacity and opportunity to address the issue.

Here the two individuals are unable to engage in horizontal forgiveness. Ds antagonistic behavior has injured T emotionally. This has instigated T to employ the mechanism of avoidance in order to cope, but she could be experiencing spiritual meltdown. No doubt, there are deep-seated issues in their lives that they have not dealt with and which are hindering their spirituality, their relationship with Christ and with each other. Nevertheless, "beneath an appearance of hatred and contempt, even beneath crime and degradation, may be hidden a soul that the grace of Christ will rescue to shine as a jewel in the Redeemer's crown"[22] Furthermore, the impasse also has a negative impact on their emotional wellbeing. However, "when the mind of man is brought into communion with the mind of God, the finite with the Infinite, the effect on body and mind and soul is beyond estimate. In such communion is found the highest education. It is God's own method of development."[23] Thus, travelling on the *road to forgiveness* has the potential of aiding emotionally-injured individuals in developing spiritually and resolving their issues.

SUMMARY

Addressing past unresolved painful issues requires at least two resources: spiritual and psychological. Some of the useful spiritual resources are intercessory prayer, the studying of Sacred Scriptures and theological reflection, while helpful psychological resources are counselling and psychotherapy. In an attempt to resolve painful issues, the process requires qualities such as boldness and maturity and is rooted in the principle which states that when we intentionally face our past painful situation and agree to address it, this enables us to engage in interpersonal forgiveness and by extension, progress towards healing.

2

THE IMPACT OF UN-SURRENDERED PAINFUL ISSUES

Water, water everywhere!

Water, water everywhere!

These were the familiar poetic rhyming words which many residents of towns and cities in South Yorkshire echoed in mid-summer of 2007. Intense downpours of rain brought about a rush of water, creating a serious situation, and saturating rural and urban areas in the region. The already high water levels of the Rivers Don and Sheaf were subjected to continuous heavy rainfall leading to all the region's rivers bursting their banks. Many areas were extensively damaged as the River Don overflowed its banks causing widespread flooding in various sections of the major city. Emergency personnel expended their energies rescuing and evacuating as many as could be helped. Individuals and animals lost their lives, while water up to 3.5 miles stretched across fields in some areas of cultivated land. And some high sports facilities were left swimming in some 1.83 m of water. The popular shopping centre was closed due to flooding with some shops remaining closed up to three months after the catastrophic meteorological disaster.

Such unwelcomed phenomenon echoes the results of situations such as sealed boiling pots, and pent-up hatred from unresolved issues. And when the situation involves the lives of human beings, the damage can be indescribable and at times ir-reparable. So what impact do un-surrendered painful issues have on hurting people? Un-surrendered painful issues tend to affect individuals in various ways, however addressing this question is based on the following principle:

When we hold onto our painful past experiences and memories, we lose opportunities for emotional and spiritual progress.

In an attempt to focus on the effect of un-surrendered painful issues on hurting individuals, I am aware of the emotional, psychological, physiological, social and spiritual impact. However, I seek to follow the second part of the methodological approach, that of applying psychological theory to the biblical perspective. By doing this, it allows me to explore the psycho-spiritual impact of interpersonal forgiveness. Thus, I share the impact on the emotional/psychological and spiritual levels.

EMOTIONAL/PSYCHOLOGICAL IMPACT

The biblical character, Jacob, had swindled his twin brother, Esau, out of the firstborn inheritance. The crafty, cunning Jacob dangled a large bowl of hot steaming soup in from of him. Then, with the need for achievement (n Ach) possibly driving his inner desires and passions, he powerfully bargained with the much needed soup and demanded the firstborn position. At that moment, the firstborn position was miles from Esau's thoughts. So he surrendered to Jacob's passionate plea by agreeing that Jacob could have his birth position in the family. By this time he had greedily taken the bowl of soup and bread from his brother's hands and devoured it.

Jacob did not only cunningly turn the birth-right over to himself, but he also deceived his blind father, by secretively pretending to be Esau. The old man had experienced a craving for wild meat, a speciality of Esau. Having been summoned to hunt down a wild animal and prepare a tasty meal, Esau dashed out of the tent. Dad was planning to pronounce a secret spiritual blessing on Esau. Accidentally, mum overheard the conversation, forcibly convinced Jacob to fetch some meat, put on some animal fur over his clothes and to take the savoury meal that she would cook to dad. Being mum's favour son and also driven by the need for affiliation (n Aff) to his mother, Jacob obediently gathered the ingredients for the meal.

It was during this brief moment that Isaac, the blind father, prayed, in full measure, the special blessing on Jacob instead. In the end, when Esau turned up, dad was so outfoxed that he didn't even have any more of the special blessing left to give Esau. This deception drove Esau to bitter and loud tears to the point that he lamented profoundly. Although dad had laid his hands on him and blessed him, Esau privately lurked in the inner recesses of his heart to persecute his crafty brother. He developed great ill-feelings for Jacob and vowed deeply that he would intentionally smite his brother with a deadly blow as soon as Isaac shut his eyes.

On hearing about Esau's revengeful plans, Rebecca, the boys' mother, advised frightful Jacob to escape to the country of her brother, Laban, and live there for a while. After some twenty year, Jacob returned to his parents' country of residence, perhaps hoping that with time, his brother would have experienced healing. It seems likely that Esau had lived with this unresolved painful situation for decades. On investigating Esau's mood, Jacob received reliable information that his brother was coming in his direction with four hundred men.[24] Who were these men? Bodyguards? A real army? Servants? What would have contributed to Esau's desire to hunt down Jacob with four hundred men even though Jacob was absent for some twenty years?

Individuals who nurse un-surrendered painful issues tend to experience anxiety in various proportions which could be dangerous to their ego. When anxiety is beyond people's coping capabilities, they tend to employ one or more techniques referred to as defence mechanism. Experiencing painful emotional issues can be traumatic, a situation which could escalate if left unresolved. From a psychological perspective, unresolved painful issues prevent people's higher order needs from being met. In fact, hurting individuals primarily focus on survival and subsistence living, thereby concentrating mainly on physiological needs such as food, water, sleep and shelter. Maslow (1955) argued that these types of deficiency needs arise because individuals have been deprived of them. Additionally, hurting individuals also seek to ensure that their safety needs are met.

Furthermore, our past hurts and experiences may be painful, but it is more important and emotionally beneficial to engage in the surrendering process than to leave the issues unresolved. The God of Heaven is interested in aiding us in experiencing spiritual renewal. That is the reason Christ, the Almighty Healer and Restorer, came to into this world. His ultimate goal was to defeat the source of all sinful deeds, thereby, helping to be released and delivered from the effects of un-Christlike attitudes and experiences, such as holding onto our painful past circumstances. This second stage of the journey is critical to how we proceed in our Christian walk and in particular, on the *road to forgiveness.*

Since individuals with un-surrendered painful issues are incapable of positively regulating the anxiety that originates from emotional problems, a vicious cycle emerges. A desire to monitor one's ego impulses arises while at the same time there are needs to be met in a stable manner, through thinking positively and rationally; and interacting and socialising with peers. Consequently, such individuals employ methods which Anna Freud (1966) identified as defence mechanisms, namely denial, repression and displacement among others. However, the absence of the emotional capacity to handle the painful issues results in emotionally-wounded individuals struggling to have their emotional needs met in a positive way. Consequently, they tend to use repression predominantly to avoid facing the issues, thereby escaping the painful issues as another means of survival.

BOX 2.1: THINKING ANALYTICALLY

Furthermore, J who is divorced and unemployed, avoids D and seeks not to be in the same environment as she is at any moment. During a counselling session with her therapist, J shares that she is very angry with D, but the emotional turmoil is impacting on her negatively. She wants to share how she really feels about the situation, but is denied the opportunity. J wears a sad countenance, sulks and complains. Moreover, she is unable to acquire a job in her area of speciality. Furthermore, her daughter, N is problematic to the point that she rebels often and ignores her mother's counsel.

Cases like the one above immediately elicit the practical questions: How can I move on with my life if my 'enemy' is unwilling to address the issue? Can I forgive someone who rejects it? Will confession to God for the part I played in the situation be sufficient? The biblical teachings on forgiveness do not indicate that forgiveness is conditional on the recipient's actions or attitudes towards the forgiver. Although she is not given the opportunity, J can extend forgiveness to D by preparing her heart for this one-way journey. Christ admonishes his followers, in his time and today, to forgive our enemies with unconditional love. Our responsibility is to forgive, in spite of the response from our perpetrator, since it determines how God will respond to us when we repent to Him in prayer.

Repressed un-surrendered painful issues portray features similar to a pumped up balloon whose air is unable to escape. With the balloon continuously being pumped up, there is danger of it exploding. Individuals who do not release painful issues, but continue to feed their undesirable feelings and attitudes about the perpetrator could soon experience distress and psychological instability, which may lead to depression and ultimately psychiatric instability.

The Encyclopaedia of Emotion, Volume 1, defines depression as an emotional state consisting of moods such as despondency, hopelessness and sadness. [25] The ICD-10 Classification of Mental and Behavioural Disorders classified depression as a disorder from which individuals are affected by issues such as depressed moods, loss of interest and enjoyment and reduced energy.[26] These mental difficulties affect the vitality of individuals, thus contributing to poor emotional wellbeing. A description of three varieties of depression is presented in Box 2.2 below.

BOX 2.2: SYMPTOMS OF VARIOUS DEGREES OF DEPRESSION		
Mild Depression	**Moderate Depression**	**Severe Depression**
• Reduced concentration and attention • reduced self-esteem and self-confidence • ideas of guilt and unworthiness • pessimistic views of the future • disturbed sleep • ideas of self-harm	• Some of the symptoms for mild depression • Considerable difficulty with social, work or domestic activities	• Considerable distress or agitation • Loss of self-esteem or feelings of uselessness or guilt • Feelings of suicide

SOURCE: Adapted from World Health organisation, *The ICD-10 Classification of Mental and Behavioural Disorders: Clinical Descriptions and Diagnostic Guidelines* (Geneva: WHO, 1992), pp.121-124.

Emotionally-struggling individuals, who employ repression as their coping mechanism for a dysfunctional relationship, could be leading a dangerous life for the long term. With anger, hatred and other negative emotions being kept sealed on the inside, such individuals tend to engage in unusual behaviours such as ostracising their friends, and withdrawing from social gatherings. Along with these unconventional actions, individuals who struggle with un-surrendered painful issues also engage in un-supported imaginations such as 'no one cares about me anymore', and 'they are all just the same'. Ellen G. White counselled that "the mind needs to be controlled, for it has a most powerful influence upon the health. The imagination often misleads, and when indulged, brings severe forms of disease upon the afflicted. … several who have brought upon themselves actual disease by the influence of the imagination."[27] Furthermore, individuals with prolonged, un-surrendered painful issues become emotionally tired as they seek to keep the issue and the perpetrator 'at bay'. In light of this, some individuals, being unable to replenish their emotional 'tank' with psychological energies necessary for functioning normally and rationally, tend to engage in abnormal behaviour. For instance, some may sleep rough on pavements or in other unconventional places, take food from the garbage bin or even display abnormal behaviours, suggesting that they are experiencing psychiatric instability.

SPIRITUAL IMPACT

Apart from the emotional/psychological impact which individuals experience from holding on to painful issues, they also tend to be impacted upon spiritually. One way by which this happens in through a display of negative attitudes and behaviours as opposed to cultivating Christian virtues. Researchers note that victims tend to experience a combination of emotions such as bitterness, fear, hostility, hatred and resentment after deliberating about a transgression, which can be categorised as a hurt or offence.[28] Furthermore, the researchers conclude that some of the basic components of an un-forgiving attitude are anger and hostility.[29] Scripture aptly instructs us about these negative emotions: "the acts of the flesh are obvious: … hatred, discord, jealousy, fits of rage, selfish ambition, dissensions, factions and envy … and the like" (Gal 5:19-20, NIV). Emerging from this list are emotional moods such as anger and emotional feelings such as hatred and jealousy, all of which have the potential to dominate our lives. Instead of focusing on Christ and seeking to progress spiritually, emotionally-injured individuals and their attackers tend to be pre-occupied with the issue and the negative repercussion.

> **When individuals hurt or offend someone, the victim tends to experience a traumatic event, primarily because he/she did not expect it. Traumatic situations produce various emotions, one of which is fear, thus the reason some people go on the 'run'.**

This points us to the ancient story of a cowboy who encountered a young lady in a restaurant. During the animated, captivating and lively conversation, the lady shared her travelling plans across a nearby river with him. On being fascinated by the young lady, the cowboy offered to take her across the river. Seeing that she was wearing a unusually long dress, he warned her that her dress would become soaked during the trip.

By now, they had started the journey. Half way across the river, the horse began to sink as it travelled. Meanwhile, the lady's multi-coloured dress began to absorb the water. On reaching the other side of the river, she complained profusely about her wet clothes and inability to find new clothes before reaching her final destination. Comforting himself, he alerted her that he had warned her about the potential situation before the trip. Upset and frustrated, she stampeded off into oblivion.

The cowboy embarked his mode of transport and returned to the restaurant. Having entered the room, he began to complain about the lady's ungratefulness. One of the men in the restaurant, being annoyed at the cowboy's attitude, alerted him that he was still 'carrying the lady' because her complaints had been bombarding his mind. On the back of that awaking piece of truth, another man advised him not to let the lady's behaviour dominate his life. Similarly, by not resolving issues, we carry them around with us and unknowingly, they tend to dominate our lives.

BOX 2.3: THINKING ANALYTICALLY

T, a graduate, and trained educator, and an active congregant, encountered a problem with a fellow congregant, which resulted in bitter tears. The impact moved her to isolate herself at every possible moment to the point where her behaviour and attitude was affecting her involvement in the life of her congregation's activities. No doubts, other individuals supported the perpetrator, based on the perspective that T needs to mature, 'grow up' and become friendly. This violently enraged and humiliated T even more, leading to an ugly confrontation with the perpetrator. She attended a session with her counsellor, during which time she complained about the issue in a raging manner.

In the discussion, she admitted that she did not want to forgive because she 'feels good' hating the perpetrator. T's demeanour changed, her attendance at religious services dipped and her involvement in the programmes of the congregation was impacted upon negatively.

In examining this case study, we can conclude that T's profound tears reveals that she has been hurt, thus causing her to move into survival mode by isolating herself, which could be impacting on her social contacts. Her main concern was survival, but also to ensure that her safety needs were met. By confronting the attacker, she seemed to be seeking to regain some 'ground' and be a powerful force with which to contend. Although this was an opportunity to assist T in seeing the dangers of remaining angry, it was an occasion when pastoral guidance could also be beneficial in an attempt to resolve the issue and bring healing to T's wounds. These goals could be accomplished through the use of resources such as intercessory prayer and further counselling sessions.

Another way individuals who hold on to painful issues are impacted upon spiritually is in their relationship with God. Jesus, in teaching His disciples how to prayer, zoomed in on the need to extend forgiveness. Matthew, a biblical writer, captured His teaching succinctly: "If you forgive those who sin against you, your heavenly Father will forgive you. But if you refuse to forgive others, your Father will not forgive your sins" (6:14-15, NLT). In spite of how religious we may be, refusing to surrender our anger and hostility and free the person of their emotional pain and agony, results in God being unwilling to extend forgiveness to our confessed sins and repentant heart. We are instructed insightfully that "nothing can justify an unforgiving spirit. He who is unmerciful toward others shows that he himself is not a partaker of God's pardoning grace. In God's forgiveness the heart of the erring one is drawn close to the great heart of Infinite Love. The tide of divine compassion flows into the sinner's soul, and from him to the souls of others. The tenderness and mercy that Christ has revealed in His own precious life will be seen in those who become sharers of His grace."[30] From a theological perspective, God values the act of forgiveness very highly among human beings. By extending forgiveness to each other, individuals portray the divine power of grace invading the evil forces that tend to be at work through the display of anger, bitterness and other negative emotional feelings.

Insightful counsel continues to advise that "it is true that he *[victim or perpetrator]* may once have received forgiveness; but his unmerciful spirit shows that he now rejects God's pardoning love. He has separated himself from God, and is in the same condition as before he was forgiven. He has denied his repentance, and his sins are upon him as if he had not repented."[31] By not recognising the need to extend mercy or display a sense of compassion, this attitude reveals our lack of understanding of and link between compassion and salvation. The divine grace which we receive compels us, who have been converted by the saving power of Christ, to be compassionate to others. Such inner expression is captured in the command to demonstrate love to each other.

Spiritual decline is another way by which individuals who continuously carry painful issues can be impacted. Being overwhelmed with the after-effects from emotional injuries, we find it difficult to prayer, study the Holy Scriptures or even attend the weekly religious services. Such an impact leads to a dip in our spirituality. "The spirit of hatred and revenge originated with Satan, and it led him to put to death the Son of God. Whoever cherishes malice or unkindness is cherishing the same spirit, and its fruit will be unto death. In the revengeful thought the evil deed lies enfolded, as the plant in the seed."[32] Added to this is the loss of meaningfulness in our worship experiences and in our prayer sessions.

The poet of Psalm73 admitted to having passed through this stage. On learning about the material prosperity of the ungodly, he was in emotional turmoil. We encounter his emotional difficulties in the following lament:

"Truly God is good to Israel,
   even to such as are of a clean heart.
But as for me, my feet were almost gone;
   my steps had well nigh slipped.
For I was envious at the foolish,
   when I saw the prosperity of the wicked.
For there are no bands in their death:
   but their strength is firm.
They are not in trouble as other men;
   neither are they plagued like other men.
Therefore pride compasseth them about as a chain;
   violence covereth them as a garment.
Their eyes stand out with fatness:
   they have more than heart could wish.
They are corrupt, and speak wickedly concerning oppression:
   they speak loftily.
They set their mouth against the heavens,
   and their tongue walketh through the earth.

Therefore his people return hither:
 and waters of a full cup are wrung out to them.
And they say, How doth God know?
 and is there knowledge in the most High?
Behold, these are the ungodly,
 who prosper in the world; they increase in riches.
Verily I have cleansed my heart in vain,
 and washed my hands in innocency.
For all the day long have I been plagued,
 and chastened every morning.
If I say, I will speak thus; behold,
 I should offend against the generation of thy children.
When I thought to know this,
 it was too painful for me;
Until I went into the sanctuary of God;
 then understood I their end.
Surely thou didst set them in slippery places:
 thou castedst them down into destruction.
How are they brought into desolation,
 as in a moment!
  they are utterly consumed with terrors.
Thus my heart was grieved,
 and I was pricked in my reins.
So foolish was I, and ignorant:
 I was as a beast before thee.
Nevertheless I am continually with thee:
 thou hast holden me by my right hand.
Thou shalt guide me with thy counsel,
 and afterward receive me to glory."
   _____ (Psalm 73: 1-24).

The language he uses depicts an emotionally-torn heart which exudes envy and grief. It portrays the ordeal of an individual who seems immensely bitter because life for him seems unfair. For example, clauses such as 'I was envious of the foolish', 'I have been plagued' and 'it was too painful' portray the profound inner pain that the Psalmist suffered on seeing immoral and unjust individuals flourishing. His reactions may seem justifiable, but it is vital for him, and us, to grasp the bigger picture which encompasses God's directive will.

The *New Living Translation* version aptly and explicitly renders the Psalmist's heart-felt experience as follows:

"Then I realized that my heart was bittr,
>   and I was all torn up inside.
> I was so foolish and ignorant—
>   I must have seemed like a senseless animal to you."
>   _____ (Psalm 73: 21-22, NLT).

Furthermore, the *Amplified Bible* version dramatically captures his inner reactions in this way:

"For my heart was grieved, embittered, *and* in a state of ferment,
>   and I was pricked in my heart [as with the sharp fang of an adder].
> So foolish, stupid, *and* brutish was I, and ignorant;
>   I was like a beast before You."
>   _____ (Psalm 73: 21-22, AMP).

A reflection on these two verses in Psalm 73 reveals apparent self-inflicted agony, hostility and turmoil, to the point that he found it difficult to accept the prosperity of ungodly individuals. Are you burning internally because your perpetrator has been released without punishment? In these first set of concluding verses, we notice the Psalmist's self-awareness emerging. He seems more reflexive and thoughtful about the difference between the path of the victim and that of the offender.

Heart-wrenching expressions such as 'my feet had almost stumbled' and 'I have cleansed my heart in vain' indicate that the poet was on the verge of turning away from God. In other words, he seemed to have struggled with his spirituality to the point that he wanted to backslide or deflect morally. Similarly, we go through such deep internal uncertainties. Life throws unexpected and unpredictable circumstances at us that can shake our faith to the core. What is impacting on your relationship with God? Have you been tempted to backslide? Have you been tempted severely to hold a grudge? How have you dealt with the raging desire to cease worshipping God because of the hurt you experienced? Taking this journey can be complex and when individuals carry un-surrendered painful circumstances, they can be impacted upon on emotional and spiritual levels.

In our moments of emotional turmoil, as a result of a hurt or an injustice, we can be comforted by the advice in Psalm 37:

Do not fret because of those who are evil
    or be envious of those who do wrong;
for like the grass they will soon wither,
    like green plants they will soon die away.
Trust in the LORD and do good;
    dwell in the land and enjoy safe pasture.
Take delight in the LORD,
    and he will give you the desires of your heart.
Commit your way to the LORD;
    trust in him and he will do this:
he will make your righteous reward shine like the dawn,
    Be still before the LORD

and wait patiently for him;
do not fret when people succeed in their ways,
　when they carry out their wicked schemes.
Refrain from anger and turn from wrath;
　do not fret – it leads only to evil.
For those who are evil will be destroyed,
　but those who hope in the LORD will inherit the land.

_____ (Psalm 37:1-9, NIV).

SUMMARY

Our emotional health, a very prominent topical issue in the twenty-first century society, is a crucial and vital aspect of our spiritual growth and personal development. However, when painful issues arise in our lives, we tend to be affected at the psychological and spiritual levels. It seems likely that carrying un-surrendered painful issues is equivalent to being unforgiving or unrepentant. However, in holding onto our painful past circumstances, we reduce the opportunity to experience emotional and spiritual growth.

3

RELEASING THE PRESSURE VALVE

The last Tuesday in the year 2006 was a dark day for many Americans. Former President, G. R. Ford had died. It was a day when all Americans were mourning. Many remembered the late President for a great act of courage, that of extending a presidential pardon to his predecessor, a former president. Political analysts and historians equally echoed that this type of treatment was in the nation's best interest. In plain terms, the late President Ford forgave the embattled President on behalf of the nation. In fact, in 1974, the Congressional-Gold-Medal recipient described the Watergate scandal as an American tragedy which could last forever. However, he deliberately and purposefully shared that if someone did not write the end to it, the scandal would continue to hang over the country's head. So, this brave and lion-hearted president resolutely concluded that the only person who could put an end to the nightmare and haunting issue was himself. Furthermore, he firmly decided that if the possibility was present, then he must proceed with the mammoth task and bring healing to his beloved nation.

This decisive president took the risk, faced America's painful situation and dealt with it by forgiving the former president. He shut a door that was haunting the Americans profoundly. The aftermath was brutal and inhumane. This courageous act cost the late President Ford dearly. His friends criticized him unmercifully. The newspapers cunningly contributed to 'turning the screws' on the negative opinions about him. He lost the 1975 elections and never became president again. But America was healed of its painful wounds.

The then serving President at the time of Ford's death remarked sombrely that his quiet integrity, common sense and instincts aided the late President Ford in bringing healing to their land and in restoring public confidence in the presidency. Terms such as a 'national nightmare', the 'greatest constitutional crisis', 'a deeply divisive time', and the 'nation's wounds' painted a picture of the America in the early 1970s. Such was the portrayal of the kind of issues which the unshakable President had to face at that time. Actually, America's political baggage had gushed into the open. It was in the public's eye. The then president inherited it. And so, in an attempt to bring about a resolution, he had to face it. In the end, peace and tranquillity cascaded across America and the nation experienced the much needed healing.

The late President Ford viewed the dire situation from a different pair of lens and was willing to release the 'pressure valve' on the Watergate scandal. Similarly, we need to reach a point in our life when can surrender the situation. By engaging in spiritual disciplines such as intercessory prayer and employing psychological resources such as counselling, the hurting individual can be helped to acquire a different perspective of their circumstances in order to move ahead with their life. How can giving up the painful issue help emotionally-hurting individuals is examined in the light of the following principle:

Reframing your difficult situation contributes to one's
willingness to surrender the painful past situation

Moreover in an attempt to address this question, I have defined the concept of reframing, examined a number of ways by which the issue can be reframed, and identified some qualities necessary for aiding us in moving successfully through the surrendering process, the second stage *on the road to forgiveness.*

REFRAMING: WHAT IS IT?

The task of reframing one's situation is seen as the principal intervention strategy which family therapists employ in seeking to "change the conceptual and/or emotional setting or viewpoint in relation to which the situation is experienced and to place it in another frame which fits the 'facts' of the same concrete situation equally well or even better, and thereby change its entire meaning. … Reframing operates on the level of meta-reality, where …change can take place even if the objective circumstances of the situation are quite beyond human control."[33] When individuals have an alternative frame of reference for their situation, it produces a new interpretation, thereby allowing them to see their "problems in a more favourable yet highly plausible light, without denying the existence of legitimate concerns."[34] Such a technique is advantageous for the emotionally- or spiritually-wounded individual since it engenders hope in him/her and also allows him/her to examine the old painful destructive issue differently.

USING THE REFRAMING TECHNIQUE

One way by which we can reframe our painful situations is to focus on Christ, the Saviour of broken and wounded human beings. The Apostle Paul, in outlining his new-found journey, had experienced the benefits of a new perspective. Scripture shares his alternative view: "I once thought these things were valuable, but now I consider them worthless because of what Christ has done. Yes, everything else is worthless when compared with the infinite value of knowing Christ Jesus my Lord. For his sake I have discarded everything else, counting it all as

The reframing technique seeks to assist clients in moving away from dysfunctional ways of thinking and to provide them with an opportunity to explore the issue through another lens.

garbage, so that I could gain Christ and become one with him. I no longer count on my own righteousness through obeying the law; rather, I become righteous through faith in Christ. For God's way of making us right with himself depends on faith" (Phil 3:7-9, NLT). That's why Paul reiterated that the things he achieved such as the knowledge of the law and his social status, he considered them to be nothing. To be lost. To be forgotten.

Moreover, the biblical writer, in seeking to move on from his past difficult lifestyle, viewed his life in a different light. Having encountered and experienced the salvific power of God, he attributed his former achievements as worthless in exchange for his new experiential journey with Christ.

The Amplified Bible Version renders Philippians 3:8 as "the priceless privilege (the overwhelming preciousness, the surpassing worth, and supreme advantage) of knowing Christ Jesus." The writer acknowledged the privileged opportunity he was given and identified his primary goal in embarking on the Christian journey, that of knowing Christ experientially by "progressively becoming more deeply *and* intimately acquainted with Him" (Phil 3:8b, AMP).

Has the situation broken, damaged or wounded you? What steps are you taking to aid you in surrendering the painful situation? What lens are you looking through in an attempt to have an alternative viewpoint? Have you stopped to consider honestly how willing you are to let go of the issue? Are you seeking intentionally to engage in the surrendering process so that you can experience some degree of healing? The journey *on the road to forgiveness* is progressive. However, it is by the grace of God that you can move forward as you reach this stage of engaging in horizontal forgiveness.

BOX 3.1: THINKING ANALYTICALLY

T, now in her forties, shared with the therapist that she desperately desired to be married so that she could start a family. She did not intend to violate the biblical principle of becoming pregnant before being married. In the six therapeutic sessions, it emerged that she had been courting a number of individuals, but each of them became married, soon after ending the relationship with her. She expressed her anger, frustration and was concerned as to the reason she was unable to maintain a relationship that leads to marriage. Moreover, she questioned her femininity and her natural attributes in order to determine whether or not these aspects of her life were faulty.

After further probing, through prayer and exploring the issues deeper with the therapist, T came to the conclusion that she has been dating and courting male companions who have had severe emotional issues, and who, on gaining emotional support from her, eventually moved on with their mended lives.

The sessions have helped her to recognise that she had been having relationships with the wrong type of male companions. In the course of the final session, she broke down in tears and admitted that she felt betrayed and 'used'. She realised from the sessions that she need to become more acquainted with potential male partners and, in her words, 'get to know their stories' before becoming committed.

The battle between T's raging negative emotions and her inner desire to lead a Christian life, while having the normal trapping of a married life embattled her. A number of issues arise in this case study. One has to do with the view that T seemed to have been holding unexpressed or high expectations of her fiancé. The following questions come to mind: Did the question of marriage ever arise in their conversations and discussions? Was she aware of any previous relationships in which these male companions were involved? Given her age, did she state her intentions immediately? What hidden psychological needs could she have been seeking to meet by engaging in various courting relationships? What types of needs could T have met for these male companions?

Another issue has to do with inhibited relationships which she has been involved in continuously. It is clear that she has not benefitted emotionally, physically nor psychologically from these relationships seeing that she has experienced betrayal. This could suggest that either the male companions had promised a lasting relationship, which did not materialise. On the other hand, it could be that she may have entered an emotional bargain with these male partners, who did not fulfil their end of the bargain. Another alternative could be that T is an emotionally difficult person to get along with, hence causing the male partners to move on to another person. A further explanation could be that T may have entered a new relationship too quickly without giving herself time to heal, thus resulting in her bringing issues of fulfilment and of broken relationships into her subsequent encounters.

Providentially, the therapy has helped her reframe the situation and although she was emotionally distraught, she has acquired a meaningful perspective of her issues. It is situations such as these that, by bringing spiritual resources to bear on the issue, they can act as an 'antidote' for the pain of the wounded. Insightfully, we are counselled that "a tender spirit, a gentle, winning deportment, may save the erring and hide a multitude of sins. The revelation of Christ in your own character will have a transforming power upon all with whom you come in contact. Let Christ be daily made manifest in you, and He will reveal through you the creative energy of His word—a gentle, persuasive, yet mighty influence to re-create other souls in the beauty of the Lord our God."[35] In essence, viewing our difficult and painful experiences in a different light aids us in being able to make emotional and spiritual progress.

Another way of reframing our painful issues is to reflect on, study and pray through the Sacred Scriptures. In fact, when we bring the God of Heaven into the situation, through prayer and the study of the Scriptures, we envision our helplessness and dependence on the God of Heaven. Such was the experience of the Psalmist David:

"My wounds fester and stink
because of my foolish sins.
I am bent over and racked with pain.
All day long I walk around filled with grief.
A raging fever burns within me,
and my health is broken.
I am exhausted and completely crushed.
My groans come from an anguished heart.
You know what I long for, Lord;
you hear my every sigh.
My heart beats wildly, my strength fails,
and I am going blind.
My loved ones and friends stay away, fearing my disease.
Even my own family stands at a distance.
Meanwhile, my enemies lay traps to kill me.
Those who wish me harm make plans to ruin me.
All day long they plan their treachery."

_____ (Psalm 38: 5-12, NLT)

While Psalm 38 describes the attacks from the writer's enemies, this portion of the psalm depicts the emotional pain he experienced during the ordeal. He admitted that he was broken and wounded, thus accounting for his severe and harsh psychological pains. Note that the language he employed in this psalm of remembrance characterises an emotionally-torn and desperate creature, who summons divine hep and seeks to 'awaken' Yahweh to his pitiful case. It is during moments like these, that having applied the various resources to our reframed situation, we can only surrender if we must honestly move forward.

The God who cares about our wounds has taken the initiative to help us reframe our struggles so that we can surrender the painful past situation. Isaiah 43 captures such a powerful admonition:

"Forget the former things;
do not dwell on the past.
See, I am doing a new thing!
Now it springs up; do you not perceive it?
I am making a way in the desert
and streams in the wasteland."
          _____(Isa 43:18-19, NIV)

We cannot help but notice the divine interest in our emotional and spiritual renewal. Here we get the distinct feeling that God passionately desires to tear away our past hurtful issues and help us to progress with our spiritual lives. He wants to bring relief and deliverance from the destructive power of the painful past issues. In essence, He desires for us to reach a place where we can connect with Him experientially and progress with our emotional healing.

BOX 3.2: THINKING ANALYTICALLY

Mrs A, a forty-five years old profession and is an active congregant of her local place of worship. She is married and has two teenage daughters, one of which is in further education and the other one has been absent from school for almost a year. She has become very frustrated on account of marital issues. Additionally, having bought a new vehicle and contributing heavily to the house mortgage, her finances and the children's health were weighing heavily on her mind. Along with these problems she had reached breaking point because of her husband's sarcastic and demeaning attitudes towards her and the children. Sometime later, she set up an appointment with her counsellor. She shared with the practitioner that the divorce was weighing heavily on her mind and she wanted 'out'. During one of the sessions, Mrs A alerted the counsellor that she wanted to attend a help centre to obtain necessary information about her entitlement as a potential divorcee.

Mrs A seems to be displaying severe desperation because of her willingness to take drastic action. Psychologically, she seems to be at breaking point, where she wants to end the marriage. This implies that her various coping strategies seemed to be ineffective. Her desire to seek legal advice at the help centre about her marital situation indicates that she was utilising a problem-focused coping strategy. Additionally, by going to her therapist, she was seeking social support for emotional issues and therefore, using this as an emotion-focused coping strategy.[36] Having explored various ways of reframing our unresolved painful issues, it is important to ensure that we possess appropriate qualities to aid us in engaging in the surrendering process.

THE SURRENDERING PROCESS: REQUIRED QUALITIES

Failing to surrender the painful issues and unresolved situations could erupt unexpectedly as was the case with the 1981 riots in England. The political landscape bent under the strains of a string of serious riots which invaded many major and prominent cities. Community Development specialists and political historians concluded that the uproar was based on race riots between communities, but were related primarily to racial tension and inner-city deprivation, a distrust of the police and central authority.

Large numbers of people from ethnic minority communities populated four main cities, where many of the residents were predominantly from the British Commonwealth. They had arrived in Britain in the 1960s and 1970s to take up low paid jobs. Furthermore, social issues such as poor housing, high unemployment and particular problems, along with racial tensions, contributed to the upheavals in the cities. Consequently, the riots emerged as a result of a spontaneous outburst of built-up resentment sparked by numerous events. Additionally, racial disadvantages and the decline of inner-city facilities and resources were some of the warning signs. Immediate action was necessary to avoid racial issues becoming a 'thorn in Britain's flesh'. Interestingly, these four major cities enjoyed decades of an affluent lifestyle. However the relocation of various types of industries and the influx of migrant workers had led to the change of the economic landscape of these cities, thereby contributing to the violence which had erupted almost un-announced.

Unlike the lack of action taken to disarm Britain's racial 'time-bomb' in the 1980s, we have to attend to the growing tension which exists in our lives. Surrendering these issues does not occur in a vacuum, but requires various qualities to propel the individual forward. Individuals, who desire to turn away from their painful past hurts and the injustice which they have experienced, are encouraged to display compassion. This quality refers to the inclination to relieve human suffering by way of being merciful or helping in a practical way or by being present to comfort the hurting. Moreover, the word 'compassion' suggests possessing a deep awareness of the suffering of another person, coupled with the wish to relieve that person's pain or plight.

BOX 3.3: THINKING ANALYTICALLY

Mrs A discussed the issue further with her counsellor and expressed the view that she needs to move on with her life. She indicated that she has been struggling with her marriage for 'years'. In the discussion, she shared that she has not been as faithful to God financially as she should have been. She is encouraged to seek pastoral help as opposed to attending the help centre where she can acquire legal advice. However, she rejected this advice on account of a diminished clergy-parishioner rapport.

In an attempt to be helped, she was encouraged to engage in spiritual disciplines such as prayer and fasting and bible studies. She showed great interest in these activities and was eager to start. On locating alternative support, she along with the helper engaged in sessions of intercessory prayer, fasting and bible studies. It was this support that helped her to view her situation through a spiritual lens when she concluded that her experiences were part of her spiritual trials which must be borne wisely.

We pause here to continue examining this case. Mrs A displays a decisive, determined and strong character, qualities necessary for this stage *on the road to forgiveness*. Evidence of her initial loss of confidence in spiritual authority is seen in her desire to consult secular organisation. Although she believed that God could help her situation, she does not state this belief explicitly. This attitude suggests that she seemed to lack the inner spiritual 'drive' to initiate contact with God, perhaps because she may not have felt as close to him as she would have wished.

The suggestion to involve God in the matter through spiritual disciplines such as prayer and fasting echoes Proverbs 3.6: "Trust in the LORD with all thine heart; and lean not unto thine own understanding. In all thy ways acknowledge him, and he shall direct thy paths." Every trial which the Christian believer encounters is beyond him/her and therefore requires divine input. However, personal effort is also necessary so that the blend of both can bring about the much anticipated victorious outcome.

In this case, I picture a caring and compassionate God, who being touched by her emotionally-destroying situation, was willing to respond to her request. The different types of support seemed to have given her a 'ray of hope' in a 'sea of desperation', thereby assisting her in re-framing the problem and seeking an alternative solution. The integration of her situation with elements of the Christian tradition reveal the importance of finding an appropriate resource to cushion the impact of sin on the holistic development of human beings. Nevertheless, the Scripture is replete with examples which demonstrate that there are some problems which can only be resolved by engaging in certain types of spiritual activities.

In relation to the required qualities, responding in a sympathetic way require individuals to display the God-given love. Scripture alerts us of Christ's command: "You have heard that it was said, You shall *love* your neighbour [sic] and hate your enemy; But I tell you, *Love* your enemies and pray for those who persecute you, to show that you are the children of your Father Who is in heaven; for He makes His sun rise on the wicked and on the good, and makes the rain fall upon the upright and the wrongdoers [alike]. For if you *love* those who *love* you, what reward can you have? Do not even the tax collectors do that? And if you greet only your brethren, what more than others are you doing? Do not even the Gentiles (the heathen) do that? You, therefore, must be perfect [growing into complete maturity of godliness in mind and character, having reached the proper height of virtue and integrity], as your heavenly Father is perfect" (Mt 5:43-48, AMP).

The repetitious reference to the word 'love' signifies the importance of displaying this quality while travelling on the road to forgiveness.

Furthermore, the theme of love also reverberates in the wisdom book of Proverbs: "Hatred stirs up contentions, but *love* covers all transgressions" (Prov 10:12, AMP). When we reflect on the verse's significance, it implies that when we display love to our offenders, it enables us to focus on developing a positive relationship with them as opposed to amplifying the painful issue which could continue to create barriers between individuals. The writer of the biblical book, 1 Peter, expanded the text as follows: "Above all things have intense and unfailing *love* for one another, for *love* covers a multitude of sins [forgives and disregards the offenses of others]" (1 Pet 4:8, AMP). Here, the use of the word *agapao,* implies the need to interact unconditionally with individuals who cause us great pain and torment us bitterly. In the command, Christ takes a radical approach in encouraging victims to take the initiative and express unconditional love to their offenders.

In displaying compassion, individuals are responding to practical theological issues such as why does the poor suffer? Does God care about the traumatised person and where is God when we hurt? This quality is a leading Christological motif played out in the lives of biblical characters and in our lives. As the human Jesus traversed along the dusty terrain of Palestinian places such as Galilee and Nazareth, many emotionally-broken, dying, sick and wounded individuals experienced the healing power of his compassionate heart. Furthermore, the destructive force of human beings elicits his empathy and awakens his zeal to eradicate evil. Whether it was the poor destitute multitude, the desperate crowd who followed him on foot, the exhausted, hunger-infested people whom he fed, the blind men who received their sight from him or the single mother whom he directed to a local church's food-bank, he enters our 'world', consoles us along the way and soothes our pain. Since the heart of God is touched by our anguish and grief, the display of his compassion through our fellow human beings is evidence of his caring character.

Imagine with me, if you will, hundreds of large multi-coloured posters strategically pinned on the lamp posts in your neighbourhood advertising you as an emotional criminal who has been on the run for a long time. It advises the surrounding communities and local businesses to stay clear of you and that they should not approach you. The posters alert the residents and your neighbours that you are dangerous, armed and could erupt or explore at any time. They provided more gritty details about you to the extent that you are angry, bitter, filled with hatred and desperately looking for revenge. Every counsellor and pastoral caregiver has put out an APB on you, with the ultimatum that you should be caught alive and be brought in to the nearest counselling office. How would you respond to this advertisement? Would you remain elusive? What qualities do you need to face the situation and give yourself in so that the situation can be resolved between you and the other person(s)?

It is essential to develop various qualities such as compassion, and courage, on realizing that the journey towards forgives can be exacting, painful and tough. Such qualities assist us in engaging in the various stages as we embark on this necessary journey.

Courage is another spiritual quality that is necessary for us to engage in the surrendering process whole-heartedly and honestly. Exhibiting courage demands a willingness to do what is right in spite of being criticised. It calls for spiritual strength to face the challenge and the impending threat from others.

We are reminded that "… if the one in danger perseveres, and in his helplessness casts himself upon the merits of the blood of Christ, our Saviour listens to the earnest prayer of faith, and sends a reinforcement of those angels that excel in strength to deliver him."[37] It is important to be aware that Christ, the

Redeemer of the human race, desires for us to overcome our painful past. Hence, displaying boldness requires us to be determined and decisive about addressing the issue so that our past negative experiences do not dominate our Christian journey.

Being empathetic is another vital attribute that we need to adopt in seeking to progress emotionally. Nevertheless, the debate surrounding this emotional attribute identifies various schools of thoughts. Authors such as Collins (1988), Miller & Eisenberg (1998), and Eisenberg, Spinard & Sadovsky (2006) contend that empathy is played out in the affective domain, whereby, an individual goes through various emotions as the result of the emergence of someone else's emotional state. For example, Mrs B, having lost her daughter in a car accident, breaks down in tears and weeps uncontrollably for weeks. However, her close friend, Mrs M, who visits her friend to comfort her and give support, on seeing her in this emotional state, assures her friend that she senses her pain. On the other hand, others such as Mackay et al. (1990) have argued that empathy is cognitive in nature, which indicates that an individual, by putting him/herself in another person's shoes, tends to engage in processes such as perspective taking and abstract reasoning in order to grasp the depth of the pain the sufferer is experiencing.

Meanwhile alternative perspectives exist alongside these two major views. Having examined the definition of empathy based on the third edition of the *Oxford Dictionary and Thesaurus*: "The power of identifying oneself mentally with and so fully understanding a person or object of contemplation, I concur with Worthington (1999) and Hoffman (2001) that empathy is a two-fold emotional attribute, consisting of affective and cognitive elements.[38] However, Feshbach (1982) and Castano (2012) propose that empathy consist of these two elements, but is also about a person possessing the capacity to grasp the views of another person.[39] Despite the extensive research on empathy, the debate remains alive, even though authors have supported one view over another, without any concrete and definitive conclusion.

Now that we have explored the nature of this emotional attribute, we notice how significant it is in the lives of emotionally-affected individuals, who are seeking to make progress and embark on *the road to forgiveness*. In order for victims and perpetrators to move pass the barrier which has been created by the painful issue, both of them need to be empathetic to each other in order to give up being harsh or hostile. When we consider the destructive nature of unresolved issues and contemplate on the severity of the un-surrendered painful experiences, we would agree that empathy should emanate from our hearts.

From a visual perspective, the diagram in Fig. 3.1 below demonstrates that the level of empathy displayed is inversely proportionate to disruptive emotions in a relationship. This

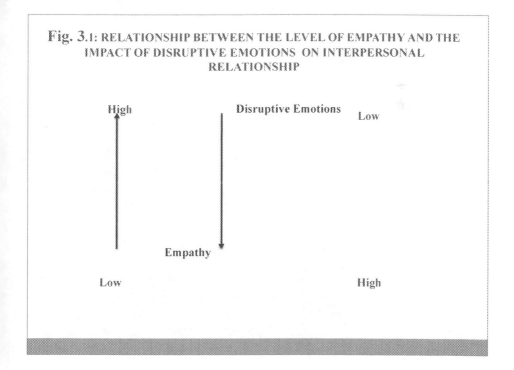

Fig. 3.1: RELATIONSHIP BETWEEN THE LEVEL OF EMPATHY AND THE IMPACT OF DISRUPTIVE EMOTIONS ON INTERPERSONAL RELATIONSHIP

suggests that the more we empathise with others, the less we would display undesirable behaviours and attitudes towards each other. This could have the potential to deepen our wounds and create disharmony.

For example, if a perpetrator walked in her victim's shoes and understood the immense pain that he had gone through because of the issue, the offender would tend to be less aggressive, bitter and less hostile towards the emotionally affected person. Moreover, sensing the victim's pain, it should move an honest offender to show compassion and be willing to address the issues, thereby repairing the fractured relationship. On the other hand, individuals who take pleasure in hurting others, tend not to be empathetic. It could be that the perpetrator has his/her own unresolved issues stored in his unconscious mind and can only act out what he possesses, which is, responding to people from a wounded heart.

BOX 3.4: THINKING ANALYTICALLY

Mrs R, a mother of three and the lone breadwinner in her matrifocal home, has had interpersonal problems with Mrs N, a member of her local place of worship for almost a decade. The impasse created deep wounds, hostility and ended with both of them not interacting at all. The issue had contributed to Mrs R resolving that she would not settle in this local congregation permanently. She was contented to come and go at will, and not be involved in the life of the congregation. However, as the situation became unbearable, she took refuge in attending another congregation, but later returned. Mrs N, on the other hand, seemed unmoved by the strain in the relationship. As time progressed, another member of the same local place of worship 'took the bull by the horn' and became the mediator between them.

In seeking to resolve the issue wholeheartedly and the fact that the local place of worship had embarked on a programme of total wholeness, Mrs. R agreed to meet her 'enemy'. Having sat both individuals down, Mrs F, the mediator, outlined the damages that the problem was causing for the local congregation and for both of them. She allowed each of them to share her views on the issues before seeking to bring about any resolution. As Mrs. R opened up and expressed her views, the tears trickled down her cheeks. Mrs F hugged her as she continued to share. She explained that she did not want to continue treating Mrs. N with bitterness and hatred.

Mrs. N took her turn and as she proceeded to share her perspective, she also broke down in tears. At that point, she faced Mrs. R and confessed that she was wrong for mistreating her and asked for forgiveness. On that note, both of them locked arms, hugged and continued weeping on each other's necks. Ten years of damage had been repaired and wounds had experienced some degree of healing in one afternoon!

A typical case such as this elicits emotional responses such as bitterness, hatred and other deep-seated destructive emotional reactions. Mrs. R seemed to have been traumatised by the problem, thus she fled for a while. The fact that she was 'on the run' emotionally and physically and seeing that she was on the periphery of the local place of worship, suggest that she had lost a sense of belonging in the congregation. Mrs N's unruffled attitude is typical of most perpetrators who hold the view that they hold the power over their victims head and therefore, become hardened and insensitive to the damage which they have caused. The above case also elicits various questions: Did Mrs. R reach a mature stage where she could face the situation? Were the two individuals compassionate towards each other? What emotional qualities were they displaying? Courage? Empathy? Openness?

Individuals such as Mrs. R and Mrs. N, who are willing to engage in the second stage of this journey, would need to display 'safe vulnerability'. A display of such a quality requires individuals to be prepared for exposure to moments of tears and pain that could accompany the act of giving up the revengeful attitude or the desire to retaliate. Such individuals require honesty, openness and also a high measure of self-awareness which would assist them in monitoring their level of maturity as they proceed to resolve their interpersonal issues. Such a quality is evident in individuals who have developed a measure of maturity to the extent that there is a resolution to accept the emotional backlash as they proceed to resolve their painful issues. In reflecting on the complexity of this journey towards forgiveness, I am cognizant that this process breaks us emotionally since defence mechanisms are not employed, neither is there a necessity for them at this stage of the journey *on the road to forgiveness.* However, it would be beneficial to invite Christ, through prayer and theological reflection into the situation and to let His sacrifice on the Cross of Calvary comfort us, soothe our pain and assist us with healing. Turning these emotionally-difficult situations over to Christ, through the use of various spiritual activities, is an important act in *on the road to forgiveness.* It is an avenue through which we can develop fruits of the spirit such as longsuffering, love and patience, thereby providing an opportunity for further spiritual maturity and emotional healing.

SUMMARY

The second stage of the journey on the road to forgiveness can be complex and heart-wrenching. It is essential for victims to reframe the issues in order to visualise the problem through another lens. Two ways by which this can be done are: making Christ the centre of your life; and using spiritual resources such as the Holy Scriptures. Having reframed our painful issues, it is also essential that we develop and display various emotional qualities such as compassion, love and also developing safe vulnerability. While there are no concrete guarantees that the process proceed uneventful, taking steps towards the ultimate goal of forgiveness is paramount.

4

EXPLORING THE MIND

A selection of linguistic entries in the third edition of *The Oxford Dictionary and Thesaurus* provide various definitions of the mind as: 1. (a) the seat of consciousness, thought, volition and feeling; (b) attention, concentration; 2: the intellect; intellectual powers; aptitude. 5: a way of thinking of feeling; 6: the focus of one's thoughts or desires; 7: the state of normal mental functioning. Such definitions provide insight into the mind from academic and emotional perspectives. When we mention the colloquial term 'mind-boggling' we are referring to something being mentally or emotionally exciting or overwhelming. Such a term produces the feeling that something will be inspiring. Here we sense that the activity is so fascinating that we are unable to express ourselves adequately, hence the personified terms such as breath-taking and hair-raising. On the other hand, the slang word 'mind-blowing' suggests that something is overwhelming, astounding, confusing, surprising or shattering. The events we experience can determine our feelings, mood and thoughts, thereby impacting on our emotional state. I wonder how an emotionally affected individual's level of consciousness can affect his/her willingness to forgive. Addressing this question requires us to focus on the following principle:

**Accepting responsibility for an adverse situation,
desiring a change of heart and working towards a
settled mind, assist with emotional progress.**

Closely associated with the above-mentioned description of positive and negative emotional states of the mind, is the three-fold structure of the mind: the conscious, pre-conscious and the unconscious sections. As we seek to embark *on this road to forgiveness*, it is important to explore the mind and provide a biblical perspective of the mind.

THE CONSCIOUS MIND

Sigmund Freud (1923) engineered the psychoanalytic theory which consisted of four major concepts, one of which is the level of consciousness. He sub-divided it into the conscious, pre-conscious and unconscious sections. These three sections contribute to the presence of an individual's experiences namely behaviours, feelings and thoughts. Using the Illustration of an iceberg, as seen in Fig 4.1, the **conscious** section of the mind, represented by the dark portion of the diagram, is equated to the tip of an iceberg, where individuals are aware of their cognitive and affective processes at that moment.

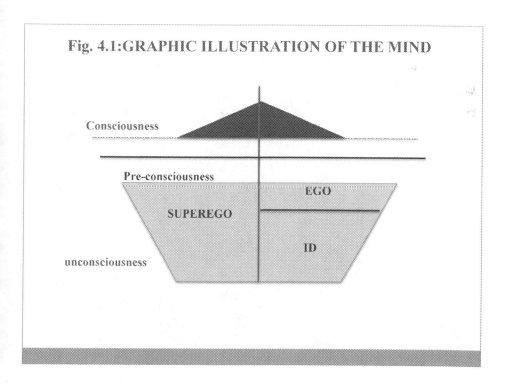

Fig. 4.1:GRAPHIC ILLUSTRATION OF THE MIND

Consciousness

Pre-consciousness

EGO

SUPEREGO

ID

unconsciousness

For example, emotionally-struggling individuals carry unresolved issues with them, and live with the pain, while the issue continuously churns in the mind. Importantly, the mental significance of representations in the conscious section could activate or hinder the mental processes taking place in the mind.[40] However, individuals, who seek to grapple with unresolved emotional issues, tend to exhibit various negative emotional moods such as being anxious, depressed and sad. Such moods need to be regulated in order to avoid negative impacts. However, being aware of the on-going emotional battle could be draining, thus leading to other ways of coping while seeking to achieve a solution.

Interestingly, "the mind controls the whole man. All our actions, good or bad, have their source in the mind. It is the mind that worships God and allies us to heavenly beings.... All the physical organs are the servants of the mind, and the nerves are the messengers that transmit its orders to every part of the body, guiding the motions of the living machinery.... The harmonious action of all the parts—brain, bone, and muscle—is necessary to the full and healthful development of the entire human organism."[41] The willingness to succeed at the second stage of this journey should be accompanied by a display of positive emotional states, which can be achieved through the reliance on various resources such as therapy and intercessory prayer.

BOX 4.1: THINKING ANALYTICALLY

D, a thirty-year old father of five, shares with his therapist that five weeks ago he has had an abusive argument with his wife and has engaged in name-calling. He seeks to engage in his normal daily duties, but over the last few days, the issues constantly stare him in the face. The words which he directs to his wife rewind in his mind almost every second. He battles with how to escape the mental anguish which he suffers and which is impacting on his social interactions outside the home.

Furthermore, he is unable to sleep, performs poorly at work and is struggling to connect with his children. One way by which he 'cashes in' on a few hours of sleep is to use the living room sofa as a temporary bed.

Logical thinking, reasoning and voluntary actions such as crying, hands- and leg-shaking also occur at the conscious level of the mind. D's situation indicates that he is operating on the conscious level, which could suggests that either something has triggered the issue and caused it to re-surface or the issue has never been allowed to enter the unconscious level of the mind. In the same way that this issue is affecting his social relationships, it would be useful to remember that "the influence of every man's thoughts and actions surrounds him like an invisible atmosphere, which is unconsciously breathed in by all who come in contact with him. This atmosphere is frequently charged with poisonous influences, and when these are inhaled, moral degeneracy is the sure result."[42] Thus, individuals with emotional issues need help in combating the negative after-effects which could be transmitted to other individuals during the process of interaction or socialisation.

THE PRECONSCIOUS MIND

In considering the preconscious section of the mind, we examine the dark portion located just below the conscious section of the mind in Fig 4.2, Freud conceptualised it as consisting of

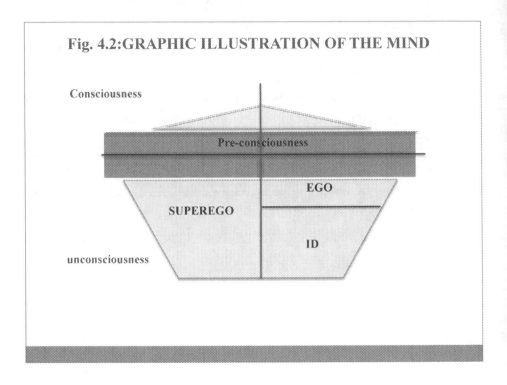

Fig. 4.2:GRAPHIC ILLUSTRATION OF THE MIND

mental states waiting to move into the conscious section of the mind, when a situation requires it. For example, in the battle between D and his wife, he attempted to remember a phrase she used to describe his attitude and admitted that the linguistic phrase was on the tip of his tongue, but he could not bring it out. This is a classic example of an idea being in the **preconscious** part of the mind and is waiting to enter into the conscious. The tip-of-the-tongue phenomenon can become more complex from a psychological perspective, in that, situations which become un-retrievable, could be as a result of a previous difficult situation becoming conscious and taking pre-eminence in the working memory of the mind. The mental materials could have undergone a form of suppression within the individual who has experienced the tip-of-the-tongue phenomenon.

Conceptually, the preconscious section of the mind consists of verbal language which is demonstrated through words and deals with actions, communications and perceptions outside of the self.[43] These mental elements are fluid between the conscious and the preconscious, in that they can pass between these two regions of the mind when individuals seek to concentrate on them. Additionally, many of our daily routines and familiar actions are located in this region of the mind. This has serious implications for individuals who are experiencing severe emotional difficulties, in that they may act in a particular way or express themselves verbally in an unacceptable way, but tend to be unaware of the consequences and effects on others.

BOX 4.2: THINKING ANALYTICALLY

C, a middle-aged single professional, is very prominent and active in her local place of worship. She is also a member of the management committee and is responsible for one of the ministries. Many of the people in her community have complained about her obnoxious attitude, and about the uncouth manner which she displays whenever she speaks to individuals.

During a counselling session, the issues come us, but C vehemently denied that she behaves in this way or speaks to people in an unacceptable way. On a few other occasions, individual members have approached C and confronted her about her attitude. In spite of these efforts, C's social relationship with others deteriorates and she has shared on a few occasions that no one appreciates her contributions to the life of religious community.

In reflecting on this case, Psychologically, C has adopted an attitude of denial perhaps because she does not want to face the reality of her behaviour or perhaps because she does not have the emotional strength, and therefore, she may not be ready to face this reality. Another reason for her engaging in denial is that she wish to perpetuate her undesirable behaviour. On the other hand, she may have perceived that her contributions to the religious group is so invaluable, that there is no way she could be acting inappropriately to other members of the community. It could be that she has been adopting an external locus, in that, the problem lies with the others and not with her.

I now revert to the earlier discussion on the mind. A major role of the preconscious region of the mind is to prevent the unpleasant emotional information in the unconscious part of the mind from rising to the surface, into the consciousness. This region holds data which we have interacted with from past experiences and learning, and afterwards have been stored away. Emotionally-distraught individuals go through various mental processes, one of which is an unwillingness to extend forgiveness to their attacker. In order for them to maintain this isolated-type of behaviour, one would ask: In which section of the mind do the mental thoughts relating to this behaviour reside? If the injured individual must be cognizant of the need to always keep the attacker at 'arm's length' and must reach the firm conclusion of not forgiving the attacker, it means that this mental attitude lies in the preconscious, waiting to be brought to the conscious. Freud contends that this region does not contain painful experiences. However, the cognitive thoughts relating to one's behaviour towards another person is based on the reality principle which guides the preconscious.

THE UNCONSCIOUS MIND

Turning now to the unconscious region, this is the area which is not available readily to the conscious which permit individuals to be aware of information. The **unconscious** is the largest section of the mind, as represented by the dark section of Fig. 4.3 below.

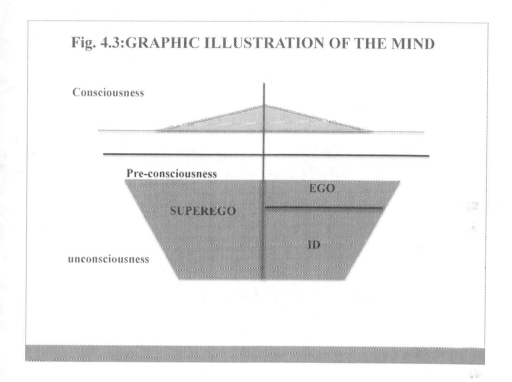

Fig. 4.3:GRAPHIC ILLUSTRATION OF THE MIND

Consciousness

Pre-consciousness

EGO

SUPEREGO

ID

unconsciousness

A major role of the unconscious is to keep inborn instinctual drives, aggressive impulses, painful or disturbing issues and hurtful emotional experiences from resurfacing into the conscious section of the mind. Freud posits the view that such experiences are repressed as a survival mechanism to avoid the emotional distress that accompanies difficult ordeals. Importantly, individuals are unable to retrieve information from the unconscious directly. It would need to be triggered by the observance of or deliberation on another painful event such as a movie about abuse or violence. Nevertheless, from a psychotherapeutic perspective, individuals, who are struggling emotionally, have the inner instinctual drive to retaliate aggressively because of the pain. However, these desires can be very dangerous and can have far-reaching consequences such as imprisonment, or the death of someone.

Thus, Freud's invention of the unconscious helps us to understand how individuals can contain the pressure from their innate drives and desires. Instead of engaging in fatal confrontations, offended individuals generally are able to act rationally and humanely at times.

BOX 4.3: THINKING ANALYTICALLY
A few months later D was invited to an emotional health conference, which hosted various workshops such as depression, and stress. He accepted the invitation and attended the seminar. As he sat engaging with the material and listening to the discussion, tears flowed down his cheeks. This was in response to the many references the presenter made to heated arguments, hating others, being unwilling to forgive and other emotionally-related issues.

Although D seemed to have deposited his past issues with his family in the unconscious section of his mind, attending the seminar heavily contributed to them being brought into conscious awareness. Here we see him reliving his pain and inner turmoil. Such experiences can be detrimental to our emotional wellbeing if we lack the resources to counteract the resurfacing of hidden unpleasant events. Thus, the need to acquire help for our conscious painful problems is essential to us experiencing healing. Furthermore, Freud also believed that when individuals repress too many emotional experiences, this could have a long-term impact such as depression or other psychological difficulties. This Freudian perspective supports the need to seek help for emotionally-threatening issues through counselling, pastoral support or psychotherapy sessions.

BIBLICAL PERSPECTIVE OF THE MIND

From a spiritual perspective, in order to engage in horizontal forgiveness, it is important that we develop the capacity to be able to place the same value on others as God imparts to them. Scripture illustrates this idea with the following verses: "Therefore I remind you to stir up the gift of God which is in you through the laying on of my hands. For God has not given us a spirit of fear, but of power and of love and of a sound mind" (2 Tim 1:6-7). The *Amplified Bible* dramatically captures this spiritual admonition in the following way: "That is why I would remind you to stir up (rekindle the embers of, fan the flame of, and keep burning) the [gracious] gift of God, [the inner fire] that is in you by means of the laying on of my hands [with those of the elders at your ordination]. For God did not give us a spirit of timidity (of cowardice, of craven and cringing and fawning fear), but [He has given us a spirit] of power and of love and of calm *and* well-balanced mind *and* discipline *and* self-control" (2 Tim 1:6-7, AMP). The biblical text portrays imagery of spiritual passion and boldness through the use of phrases such as 'stir up the gift', 'laying on of hands' and 'spirit of timidity'. Emerging from this is the need for the offended and perpetrators to address their spirituality in order to take on the challenge of facing the disturbing issues in their lives.

I want to take a look at the interconnection among 'timidity', 'power', 'love' and 'well-balanced mind'. In being inspired by the Holy Spirit and allowing Him to guide our path as we engage in our daily plans, Christian believers need to adopt the perspective that weakness does not feature in any stages of life-transforming events such as conversion or baptism. Additionally, reference to 'power' or spiritual strength indicates that this quality is necessary for taking the journey on the road to forgiveness, hence the reason we cannot be timid. Furthermore, we cannot express hateful attitudes towards each other. Since this attitude is not from the Divine One, its source would have to be the evil one. Thus, when we display love to others through spiritual strength, these qualities help individuals to develop better feelings and thoughts towards their enemies. Also, in applying these spiritual qualities while we are on this journey, the offended and attackers are encouraged to develop courage and stand up to the difficult situation in Christ's power in order to make progress. It is important that we are not chased by inner fear or not made to feel ashamed about our emotional struggles, but be determined to experience healing.

The above biblical texts signal that there are practical things we must do to aid us in acquiring Christian qualities as we prepare for horizontal forgiveness and heal the pain which has emerged from broken relationships. That's the reason the biblical book of Romans declares: "I appeal to you therefore, brethren, *and* beg of you in view of [all] the mercies of God, to make a decisive dedication of your bodies [presenting all your members and faculties] as a living sacrifice, holy (devoted, consecrated) and well pleasing to God, which is your reasonable (rational, intelligent) service *and* spiritual worship. Do not be conformed to this world (this age), [fashioned after and adapted to its external, superficial customs], but be transformed (changed) by the [entire] renewal of your mind [by its new ideals and its new attitude], so that you may prove [for yourselves] what is the good and acceptable and perfect will of God, *even* the thing which is good and acceptable and perfect [in His sight for you]" (Rom 12:1-2, AMP).

Christians virtues and qualities such compassion, graciousness, humility and long-suffering are vital to assist the injured and the offender in taking the journey of forgiveness.

Here we are admonished to engage in four things: 1) yield, to the God of Heaven, our thoughts and entire being which must be wrapped in devoted service and be prepared to engage in true spiritual worship. In order for emotionally-affected individuals to experience God meaningfully in worship, they would need to prepare their heart through confession and repentance; (2) not to adopt the behaviour of the world such as nursing hatred and keeping grudges; (3) undergo an inward spiritual transformation by having new motives towards each other, attained only by the transforming power of God's grace and love; (4) discern experimentally those attitudes and behaviours which please God who seeks to lead all individuals to repentance, thereby accepting the salvific sacrifice of Christ.

These four actions provide insightful themes in relation to developing positive emotional states necessary for engaging in horizontal forgiveness. The first theme relates to the interconnection between the words 'dedicate' and 'devote' as are expressed in the *Amplified Bible* version. Positive emotional states such as being calm, elated or satisfied do not occur automatically. We must be willing to surrender to God and seek to lead a life which can bring glory to the His name. As we seek to dedicate our lives through times of prayer and reflection, this aids with the daily sanctification every believer should engage in, and by extension, signalling that we are at God's disposal to use for His honour. This suggests that hurting individuals and the injurers are encouraged to address the unresolved issues and painful problems in their lives in order to progress spiritually.

Second, the words 'sacrifice', 'service' and 'worship' reveal an interconnection, in that, within the context of the Romans 12:2, Christian believers lay themselves on their 'altar' of daily prayer and devotion, indicating that they give their entire being as an offering. By bringing ourselves to God as a tangible offering, we are engaging in worshipping the Creator of the universe. Such an existential experience would be impossible when bitterness and hatred among other negative emotions are present in our being. Thus, this implies that unless we resolve those painful issues, our worship and service to God are meaningless.

Importantly, the act of worship is very significant. Evidence of this is seen when Christ made reference to it ten times in an extensive encounter between Himself and the woman at the well: "Our forefathers *worshiped* on this mountain,... Jerusalem is the place... to *worship.* Jesus said to her, Woman,... you will *worship* the Father neither in this mountain nor in Jerusalem. You [Samaritans] do not know what you are *worshiping.* We do know what we are *worshiping,* for [after all] salvation comes from [among] the Jews...., when the true (genuine) *worshipers* will *worship* the Father in spirit and in truth (reality); for the Father is seeking just such people as these as His *worshipers.* God is a Spirit (a spiritual Being) and those who *worship* Him must *worship* Him in spirit and in truth (reality)" (John 4:19-24, AMP). *Worship* is a key aspect of our spiritual experience with God. It transcends the attendance at a religious service and transports us into a time of adoring God through His Spirit, with His power, with enthusiasm, from the heart and with the right motives, as opposed to tradition. Such frequency signifies the importance of *worship* and reinforces its significance in our Christian life. Importantly, true worship positions us in the submissive/directive will of God, whereby we please Him. Furthermore, in order to worship the Creator whole-heartedly, it is important that we address any negative attitudes, habits or thoughts which we may be holding on to in our life.

SUMMARY

In addressing unresolved painful situations, individuals would benefit from an understanding of the impact of such issues of the mind. In particular, it would be advantageous for this category of people if they are aware of the three basic levels of consciousness namely the conscious, preconscious and unconscious. Additionally, the biblical view of the mind signals the need for individuals to display courage and think positively, thereby valuing individuals as created being who should be loved unconditionally. Moreover, in developing a settled and peaceful mind, our spirituality improves and our relationship with God becomes experiential, more meaningful and purposeful.

5

THE BATTLE IS IN THE MIND

K, a single mother, who is now retired, had her only child during her late teens. It was an era when her poverty-stricken family could only afford subsistence living. Their financial saviour was a few plots of agricultural land which her parents rented from the plantation owners. Various agricultural products such as carrots, potatoes and sugarcane competed for the valuable space. In spite of this financial 'drop in the bucket', K experienced a harsh life, especially at the hands of her Christian mother. On realising that K was pregnant, her mother banished her from the family home, with the view that she would bring embarrassment and shame to the already suffering family. It meant that the distraught K had to travel on her all-fours to seek accommodation from neighbours and distant relatives.

As time elapsed, the young inexperienced mother managed to secure work, which allowed her to acquire a baby-sitter, so that she could earn her own finances to care for her baby. Difficulties continued where some of her relatives, who pretended to be supporting her, were actually, ciphering off her much-needed funds which was hidden in the house. On reaching middle age, she nervously reflected on the harsh inhumane treatment which she helplessly experienced at the hands of her mother and concluded that her now-deceased mother does not deserve her forgiveness.

Her moments of reflection brought to the surface many hurtful and painful experiences she had suffered over the years from various members of her family. Some of these experiences include her parents' unwillingness to provide the tuition fees for her schooling; siblings controlling her newly-bought house during her late twenties; some of them subtlety demanded that she baby-sit their children; and a few others prevented her from attending work, thus jeopardizing her job with her employer. With all of these painful issues etched on her mind, K repeated many of these experiences every time the name of her mother or some of her siblings were mentioned. She frequently functioned in the rehearsal mode during which time she would announce a catalogue of transgressions she had suffered during her early life.

One situation seems certain for K and that is, there is a battle in her mind. This experience and other similar ones indicate that un-forgiven painful issues do not heal, they fester. I pose the question again: How can an emotionally affected individual's level of consciousness affect his/her willingness to forgive? In addressing this question, I will seek to provide four perspectives on the view that the battle is in the mind. At the outset, this chapter is built on the same principle as that of Chapter 4. In reviewing the principle, we are reminded that by

Accepting responsibility for an adverse situation, desiring a change of heart and working towards a settled mind, we can be assisted with emotional progress.

FIRST PERSPECTIVE: IMPACT OF UNCONSCIOUS MATERIAL

First, I turn to Freud's perspective of the unconscious section of the mind. He argued that our behaviours are influenced by deeper issues in our lives which lie dormant and at times remain unexplained. Added to this, is the fact that the unconscious is the repository for people's desires, feelings and other emotional material. Moreover, painful experiences and unpleasant memories occurring in the early years of our lives become buried through repression. This perspective provides an understanding of how individuals, such as K in the above-mentioned case study, tend to be impacted upon negatively

Researchers in the field of psychoanalysis identify various types of repression such as primary repression and secondary repression, where primary repression involves blotting our unconscious emotional elements

71

such as desires and urges which have never been brought into the conscious.[44] Individuals who seek to bury emotional material which may cause an original issue to resurface is seen as engaging in secondary repression.[45] Both types of this defence mechanism are techniques which emotionally-distraught individuals employ to conceal the real situation occurring in their mind.[46] Thus, it provides them with an avenue by which they can handle painful information without being intimidated psychologically.

Different schools of thought provide perspectives about repression. Some authors (Cramer, 2000; Blackman, 2004; Rassin, 2005) believe in the unconscious nature of repression, while other such as Anderson and levy (2002) argue for a conscious state. Having dealt with various practical theological issues over the years and observed how individuals deal with their pain, I support the view that repression is a conscious state. This position is taken based on the view that for individuals to survive emotionally, they make a conscious choice to blot out the unpleasant memory from the foreground of their mind. Alternatively, authors such Erdelyi (2001) contend that repression can be either conscious or unconscious. Consequently, proponents of an unconscious state refer to this as suppression, a mechanism which individuals knowingly employ in order to conceal painful thoughts and events from the conscious section of the mind.

BOX 5.1: THINKING ANALYTICALLY

K, on becoming a mature adult, experienced a very traumatic situation when her fiancé was killed untimely and in a very horrific manner. One day, while at work, she received the news, which overwhelmed her tremendously. She succumbed to the emotional pressure and suffered a psychiatric disorder which lasted for most of her adult life. To add 'salt to her wounds', she unwillingly was given to her mother to be 'cared' for until her 'recovery'. By this time she had had two major life-changing circumstances on her hands.

Issues such as this one, produce many complex questions. Did K's upbringing prepare her for life's difficulties? Had K overcome the first tortuous experience with her mother? Did K have the emotional capacity to deal with the second situation? Why did the informers not prepare her for the traumatic news? This case illustrates the difficulties surrounding the battles we face in life and the ones we fight in our minds. The manner in which we overcome them and experience healing on the way, relates to how we address the painful experiences in the various levels of our consciousness. The deeper the unresolved pain, the more difficult it is to engage in horizontal forgiveness.

SECOND PERSPECTIVE: EXISTENCE OF INTERNAL SPIRITUAL BATTLE

There is also an internal spiritual battle constantly taking place in the mind. The biblical writer of the book of Romans writes: "So I find this law at work: although I want to do good, evil is right there with me. For in my inner being I delight in God's law; but I see another law at work in me, waging war against the law of my mind and making me a prisoner of the law of sin at work within me. What a wretched man I am! Who will rescue me from this body that is subject to death? Thanks be to God, who delivers me through Jesus Christ our Lord! So then, I myself in my mind am a slave to God's law, but in my sinful nature, a slave to the law of sin" (Rom 7:21-25, NIV). Hurting individuals, in dealing with wrongs against them are in fact contending with sinful issues which continuously and aggressively bear down on their emotional capacity to be compassionate and kind.

Paul, the biblical writer of the above biblical text, reiterates the conflict between the law of God and the law of sin by observing that "those who live according to the flesh have their *minds* set on what the flesh desires; but those who live in accordance with the Spirit have their *minds* set on what

73

the Spirit desires. The *mind* governed by the flesh is death, but the *mind* governed by the Spirit is life and peace. The *mind* governed by the flesh is hostile to God; it does not submit to God's law, nor can it do so" (Rom 8:5-7, NIV). In this context, the mind, which refers to 'our way of thinking' can be controlled by worldly attitudes, behaviours and thoughts. On the other hand, it can be governed by God's spirit which produces life and peace. Such existential tension also mirrors the anxiety we experience when faced with unresolved issues. Ellen G. White remarks that "few realize the power that the mind has over the body. A great deal of the sickness which afflicts humanity has its origin in the mind and can only be cured by restoring the mind to health. There are very many more than we imagine who are sick mentally."[47] This suggests that in order for us to travel *on the road to forgiveness* successfully, we must seek to address the emotionally-distressing battle in our minds.

Furthermore, Paul, the biblical writer, reiterates the conflict between the law of God and the law of sin by relating it to the concept called a 'way of thinking'. In focusing on the repetitious use of the word *phroneo* and its derivatives in Romans 7, we recognize its significance to our attitude to others. The way we think has an effect on how we relate to others and by extension, how we treat them emotionally. Human beings, having been born into a world of sin, are subjected and pre-disposed to display sinful habits. Thus, from a biblical and theological perspective, one's way of thinking is influenced generally by universal evil.

The concept of 'the mind' provides a thematic thread particularly through the book of Romans, the main New Testament book which addresses systematic theological topics such as sinfulness of human beings and sanctification. Here the idea of disposition, frame of mind, outlook or mind-set emerges. It relates to what we are thinking and the motive behind our thoughts. Furthermore, our way of thinking points to the way we view people. When we consider this view, we must ask: How can we develop a positive disposition to others? What activities are we engaged in to develop a Christ-centred mind? Does our way of thinking contribute to a negative impact on others?

BOX 5.2: THINKING ANALYTICALLY
S, a young adult, lives with her parents, all of whom worship at the denomination in which they grew up, along with the grandparents. S decided to change denominations, a decision which infuriated her parents. In order to keep her from attending the worship services of this new place of worship, her parents changed the locks and kept everything 'under lock and key'. As time progressed, they put S under 'house arrest' which meant that she could only leave the house when they were going out. The food in the refrigerator and in the cupboard were also under 'lock and key', therefore, prohibiting her from cooking. Furthermore, since she longed to worship with her new community of believers, she escaped through a window. On knowing about it, her parents evicted her. S became angry, in tears and refused to communicate with her parents.

It is certain that S is hurting from the emotional difficulties she had been experiencing with her parents. Should S take the initiative and forgive her parents? Do the parents have the right to mistreat S? Are there any conditions necessary to help S forgive her parents? How would the experience impact on her level of consciousness and can she surrender the painful issues?

The experiences of K and S remind me of the importance and the role of the family as a social institution. It is in the family setting that one's personality is developed and nurtured. Members are trained and prepared for life outside the home. Here, we wrestle with different personalities and have the opportunity to adapt according to the different types of people we encounter. Family provides a cushion for life's challenges, where everyone tends to bring their resources together in an effort to provide the needed assistance.

The role of the family reminds me of a heart-stirring biblical story of a desperate mother whose daughter was controlled and overpowered by a demonic spirit. We can imagine the various emotional and physical struggles this daughter was experiencing. The distraught state of the daughter instigated the mother to become anxious, frantic and persistent. Perhaps, in the mother's desperation, she searched her community for help. She may have tried various resource personnel. But then, an extraordinary day came. Jesus, along with His disciples, journeyed through her community. Certainly, it was unexpected for the residents of this community. As Jesus and His disciples approached the entrance of the community, the mother rushed up to Jesus begging Him to help the limped daughter. This was an illustration of compassion being played out from the heart. What drove this mother to seek help for her demon-possessed daughter? What would cause you to make an unusual sacrifice for a hurting individual?

While an animated and deep theological discussion occurred between Jesus and the disciples, the mother was pushing her case. She begged. She pleaded. She fell on her knees. Her heart must have yearned to see a healed daughter. Jesus paused. The disciples discussed extensively whether to allow the hurting mother to benefit from some of their resources. They deliberated on whether they should let her into their community. They probably felt that they were the gate-keepers! As she remained on her knees, Jesus looked intently at the determined mother. His heart reached out to hers. And then he pronounced the healing command. In what ways is your family life assisting you in developing emotionally? Is your family dysfunctional? What type of relationship do the members in your family have? Compassionate? Normal? Peaceful? Stormy?

On returning to the biblical text in Romans 7, I reflect on the clause 'waging war against the law of my mind'. It epitomises the emotional battle which individuals with painful situations endure. So what emotional battles are you fighting at present? With whom are you fighting? Your children? Fellow church member? Neighbour? Spouse? Apart from these types of battles, we also engage in mental battles. We fight in our minds with an antagonistic colleague, a harsh professor or even an uncompassionate pastor. Although our minds may be engulfed with battles, it is essential to work towards surrendering our painful past in order to move towards extending forgiveness. This process becomes important since "the condition of the mind affects the health to a far greater degree than many realise. Grief, anxiety, discontent, remorse, guilt, distrust all tend to break down the life forces and to invite decay and death."[48] The link between our emotional progress and the mind therefore, highlights the need to embark on each of the stages of this important journey *on the road to forgiveness.*

I pause at this time to consider the significance of 'the law'. It conjures up in our mind, the idea of divine directives and statutes. The law ensures that justice and fairness are played out in our lives. It is true that life is not fair, but when we attempt to apply the law of God to our daily affairs, a sense of justice emerges. This reminds me of the divine promise which the prophet Jeremiah captures: "But this is the new covenant I will make with the people of Israel on that day," says the Lord, "I will put my laws in their minds, and I will write them on their hearts. I will be their God, and they will be my people" (Jeremiah 31:33, NLT). Living a life guided by God's law assists us in reaching the stage in our life when we can deal with our pain and refuse to seek revenge.

The law also requires individuals to display the fruit of the spirit such as love, patience, kindness and long-suffering, thereby valuing each other highly. More importantly, the law of God provides a moral compass for the injured and the offenders

The Law and the Holy Spirit operate with one aim: To aid individuals in experiencing peace and being in God's directive will.

who, in making choices, must be aware of the impact that could be made on their future relationships.

Each of us is plagued with the spiritual battle in our mind between the law of God and the law of sin. Some individuals give in to this battle, thereby emitting various types of attitudes. Let's ponder on a few things: Are you hurting emotionally? Have you been spiritually abused? Emotionally abused? How willing are you to extend forgiveness? Have you been struggling to live by God's law while interacting with others? To what degree have your wounds been healed?

It is important to note that your degree of healing determines your willingness to forgive. For instance, individuals who are in pain and are hurting tend to utter the following popular words: "I will never forgive him." These five deadly words are the frequent sentiment of individuals who are unable to overcome a hurt or a scandal. It does not matter the state of some victims. They seem determined to hold the perspective. This brings to mind the case of a young man suffering from a rare type of cancer. "I will never forgive him." These were the death-bed confessional words of a terminally-ill forty-seven year old son of an imprisoned embezzler. His father, a former investor, 'creamed off' billions of dollars from his clients. The young cancer patient had been travelling a long road paved with treatment such as chemotherapy, radiation and a transplant. Even though the transplant was showing signs of failing, the struggling patient vowed not to forgive his father. The family's problems heightened when his brother committed suicide. And the older son's unwillingness to extend forgiveness was reinforced because the fraud had occurred under their 'noses' and they were unaware of their father's illegal financial activity.

How can the injured reach a place where they are willing to forgive? And what about the offender? Offenders tend to be uncompassionate and inhumane in their attitude and behaviour towards their target. Unless they are helped with and held accountable for their deeds, they will strike again like a venomous viper. Their behaviour seems to follow an old maxim: 'you can only give out what you have'. Individuals who are hurting others could also be experiencing their own emotional turmoil. However, they tend not to seek help, but prey on others and project the emotional difficulties on them.

THIRD PERSPECTIVE: DEVELOP AN APPROPRIATE FOCUS

So far we recognise that the battle in the mind can be intense, demanding and overwhelming at times. However, the advice aptly provided is to: "set your minds *and* keep them set on what is above (the higher things), not on the things that are on the earth" (Col 3.2, AMP). The third perspective is that we should seek to have an appropriate focus which aids with our emotional and spiritual maturity. The Psalmist David shares one way to achieve such a focus:

Blessed *are* the undefiled in the way,
　　Who walk in the law of the LORD!
Blessed *are* those who keep His testimonies,
　　Who seek Him with the whole heart!
They also do no iniquity;
　　They walk in His ways.
You have commanded *us*
　　To keep Your precepts diligently.
Oh, that my ways were directed
　　To keep Your statutes!
Then I would not be ashamed,
　　When I look into all Your commandments.
I will praise You with uprightness of heart,
　　When I learn Your righteous judgments.

I will keep Your statutes;

Oh, do not forsake me utterly!

How can a young man cleanse his way?

By taking heed according to Your word

With my whole heart I have sought You;

Oh, let me not wander from Your commandments!

Your word I have hidden in my heart,

That I might not sin against You.

Blessed *are* You, O LORD!

Teach me Your statutes.

With my lips I have declared

All the judgments of Your mouth.

I have rejoiced in the way of Your testimonies,

As *much as* in all riches.

I will meditate on Your precepts,

And contemplate Your ways.

I will delight myself in Your statutes;

I will not forget Your word."

_____ (Psalm 119:1-16).

Can you envisage the prevalent imagery of an obedient heart in the Psalm? Have you recognised how significant the Word of God is in preserving an obedient heart? Have you observed how the writer deliberately and intentionally employs different synonyms to describe God's law which require obedience? How he places great value on God's Word? What would help you gain the focus you need? How can your mind be more spiritual?

> **The law of God guides the relationship between Him and human beings. At the same time, the law governs the interaction between individuals.**

This portion of Psalm 119 reflects the general nature of the entire psalm whose central theme is the 'law' which "is the good news of the Lord's intervention. It promises the healing of broken relationships and provides a guideline for human conduct."[49] Nevertheless, the words relating to the 'law' can be sub-divided in the following way: promise, word and 'ordinances', where these words deal with "the Lord's promise or assurance to humans and to his deeds of salvation"[50] On the other hand, the other group: 'decree', 'precepts', 'statutes' and 'commandments' captures "God's instruction to humankind and can be as a norm for our actions."[51] Thus, in focusing meditatively on, studying and applying God's instructions, we gain a means by which we can handle the battle in our mind, thereby experiencing emotional and spiritual progress.

Isaiah also contributes to the perspective of having a focus by expressing one of God's desires for our emotional health: "You will guard him *and* keep him in perfect *and* constant peace whose mind [both its inclination and its character] is stayed on You, because he commits himself to You, leans on You, *and* hopes confidently in You" (Isaiah 26:3, AMP). The declaration indicates the certainty with which the prophet Isaiah speaks. Divine protection is guaranteed so that we can form Christ-like views and thoughts about others. The journey *on the road to forgiveness* can be long and therefore, we are encouraged to trust in God. We are encouraged to allow Him to lead us on this journey, lean upon and depend on Him, so that our mind may not be engaged in unending and painful battles.

Let's focus on the connection between the two ideas 'keeping us in perfect peace' and 'whose mind is stayed on God'. Reference to the word 'peace' conjures up the idea of health, happiness and prosperity, implying the extensiveness of the peace which God desires to bestow on individuals. Our peace originates with Christ, the comforter and healer of the injured. The theme of 'peace' prevails in the book of Isaiah. The following text provides an example:

"For to us a child is born,
 to us a son is given,
 and the government will be on his shoulders.
And he will be called
 Wonderful Counsellor, Mighty God,
 Everlasting Father, Prince of Peace.
Of the greatness of his government and peace
 there will be no end.
He will reign on David's throne
 and over his kingdom,
establishing and upholding it
 with justice and righteousness
 from that time on and for ever.
The zeal of the LORD Almighty
 will accomplish this."

     _____ (Isaiah 9:6-7, NIV).

This section of Isaiah 9 depicts the nature of Christ, with Him being an advocate of mankind's serenity. Such a role seems to suggest that He ensures that individuals overcome battles, be they emotional, psychological or spiritual, thereby ensuring that we are in harmony with each other. However, this type of peace can only be achieved when our mind becomes focused by dwelling on God's teaching. Actually the type of peace God gives is vital to the mind, to the extent that as our way of thinking is influenced directly, our emotional wellbeing will improve. Are you at peace with yourself? With your colleague? Employees? Fellow church member? A sibling? A relative?

FOURTH PERSPECTIVE: DISPLAYING AGAPE LOVE

We now turn to the fourth perspective which is summed up in this verse: "And He replied to him, You shall love the Lord your God with all your heart and with all your soul and with all your mind -intellect). This is the great (most important, principal) and first commandment. And a second is like it: You shall love your neighbor as [you do] yourself" (Mt 22:37-39, AMP). In loving God, we are encouraged to respond to His directives regarding our treatment of each other by observing and upholding His commandments, which helps us to respond compassionately to everyone. Based on this perspective, we see the significance of the Decalogue, where the first four commandments relate to the God-human relationship.

Additionally, our love for God is displayed through our worshipping Him as the only true deity. In worshipping Him, we express our affection for His Name and Nature by honouring, respecting and lifting Him beyond the human realm. When the mind is entangled in painful unresolved emotional battles with each other, worshipping God becomes almost impossible, thus our spiritual maturity is affected negatively.

Also, our love for God is displayed through Christ-centred service to humanity by using the different gifts which he has bestowed on us. Christ, in teaching His disciples, enforced the need to show love for each other. The way we interact with each other portrays the depth of our affection towards each other. Since the love of God which should reflect from us, to each other is unconditional, it is important to seek ways by which we can reach out to others and be at peace with them unconditionally.

BOX 5.3: THINKING ANALYTICALLY

L, a forty-year old professional, recounted her personal mental battle with her mother who was young and inexperienced when she gave birth to L. She shared with her therapist that she became aware of various family secrets over the years, one of which was her lack of paternal information. On being aware of this, she constantly attacked her mother, demanding to know all about him.

With these demands bringing back mum's long time pain and anguish which she suffered during the pre- and post-natal stages of L's life, mum attempted to avoid providing this painful information. L's unhappiness grew. Her resentment for her mother deepened and eventually was extended to her numerous siblings.

The hatred developed to the point that they had no 'normal' contact like other families. L became distraught to the point that the performance on her job was deteriorating. She began asking numerous questions: 'How can I love a mother like her?' 'What is she hiding?'

Christ's admonition to love our neighbour in the same way that we love ourselves is the basic principle that creates harmony between individuals. However, cases such as this one propel us to question our belief system, the power of prayer and God's existence. When we reflect on L's experience, we notice that the love for her mother became conditional, reaching a point where she appeared to be withholding affection from her mother. It is true that 'the love of Christ compels us', however, L's pain seem to be holding her back. Is horizontal forgiveness possible in this case? Does L have the resources to help her face the issue? Has mum been healed from her pre-natal ordeal? Should L forgive her mother and experience progress with her life? How can L be healed from the impact of this situation? Although it is important to express unconditional affection to each other, past painful unresolved issues hinder the expression of such qualities, thereby retarding our healing process.

SUMMARY

Past unresolved painful issues create battles in our minds. Nevertheless, the unconscious is impacted upon severely by painful experiences which can only resurface when triggered by the individual contemplating deeply on another similar experience. Unpleasant information tends to be hidden either through repression or suppression, two popular defence mechanisms used by adults. In discussing repression, three perspectives prevail: a conscious, unconscious and a mixture of the two views. We also experience a perpetual spiritual battle in our mind between God's law and sin, a situation which can be counteracted if we focus on Christ-centred issues. Thus, an essential quality which can assist us in developing such a focus is to express unconditional love to each other, just as God loves us unconditionally.

6

LEAVE YOUR PAINFUL
PAST IN THE PAST

Dawn had arrived after wrestling with the still darkness of the previous night! It was the beginning of daylight. The first light of the day was now appearing. The sunrise was about to break forth. The clouds were rolling back gradually and slowly to allow the sunlight to spread its wings across the earthly terrain. In the meantime, excited crowds of people speedily gathered at the Jerusalem temple to listen intently to special messages. And then there was an interruption. Unbelievable! Incredible! Incredulous!

Men from the main Jewish groups trampled courageously and graciously up the temple steps and brought a trembling lady into the building. They viciously demanded that she stand in the middle of the captivated congregation. Then they unsympathetically exposed her. These passionate, zealous religious leaders broadcast her evil deeds throughout the temple. It was scandalous! Then they insisted that the religious speaker put her on trial, judge her and execute punishment on her immediately.

Perhaps being shocked by such uncompassionate and inhumane behaviour, silence prevailed. He simply knelt to the ground and began writing imaginary inscriptions. The Jewish accusers insisted that the woman be judged and convicted. Then he looked up gradually and explained that if any of them was innocent, then that person should be the one to punish the woman. Immediately, the Jewish religious leaders released their icy grip and backed off one by one. With their heads held down in shame, they disappeared without a trace.

There in the middle of the congregation, the pitifully accused lady remained alone. The religious speaker then inquired as to where her accusers had disappeared to so quickly. Having, declared her lack of knowledge about them, he compassionately encouraged her to return to her community, turn away from her former lifestyle and to live a respectful life. On turning away from the 'judgement' room, he reminded her not to go back to that type of life: 'Go your way and keep away from evil practices.' These words seem to convey the following message: 'leave your past lifestyle in the past'; 'the past is the past'; 'do not go back to that old lifestyle'; or that 'the past has gone so don't go back to it'.

On reaching the third stage of the journey *on the road to forgiveness,* the communique seems to be clear: leave your painful past in the past. But there is a rebounding question: how do we let the past painful issues remain in the past so that we can complete the journey? In pondering on this question, it is important to note that this third stage of the journey consists of three steps, which are incorporated into the principle on which this chapter is built:

Emotionally let go of the past painful issues by discerning the hindrances to your progress, discovering and pursuing a Christ-directed goal.

The above-mentioned principle guides us into the third stage of the journey *on the road to forgiveness,* that of leaving the painful past in the past. We have now reached the

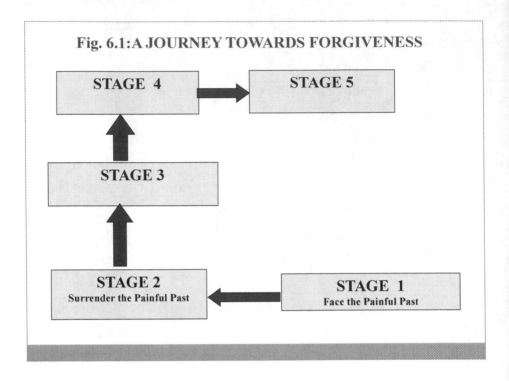

Fig. 6.1:A JOURNEY TOWARDS FORGIVENESS

STAGE 4

STAGE 5

STAGE 3

STAGE 2
Surrender the Painful Past

STAGE 1
Face the Painful Past

mid-point of this journey. It is at this junction that decisions need to be made. This part of the journey brings us to a cross-road because we need to leave the past in the past so that we can make emotional and spiritual progress. In examining this process, the following three steps are discussed below: (1) discerning hindrances; (2) discovery of a Christ-centred goal and (3) focusing on the new goal.

STEP 1: DISCERNING HINDRANCES

The willingness to move on from a difficult situation requires pinpointing those areas of our life that are affecting us negatively. One way to identify those dark areas in our lives is to deliberate intentionally on where we are emotionally and engage in personal assessment of our emotional health. Reflective questions such as the following are useful: what aspect of my painful past is affecting me? How am I handling this difficult issue? What do I need in order to let go of that issue which could be keeping me back? Employing these searching questions should be accompanied with the desire to deal with the responses that emerge from the introspection.

In using the experiences of the Apostle Paul, a biblical character, Scripture chronicles this part of his journey for us: "But whatever were gains to me I now consider loss for the sake of Christ. "What is more, I consider everything a loss because of the surpassing worth of knowing Christ Jesus my Lord, for whose sake I have lost all things. I consider them garbage that I may gain Christ" (Phil 3:7-8, NIV). We noticed that Paul, in examining his personal difficulties, recognised the things that were hindering him. On recognising the destructive nature of his social status, religious heritage and family background, he set about to make drastic changes. He made a conscious decision, through the power of the Holy Spirit, to 'lose' the hindrances in his life. In order to arrive at this stage in our journey, it is important to engage in a season of confession, repentance and soul-searching, thereby allowing Christ to wash us in His blood. Just as the Apostle Paul gave up the once-cherished achievements and possessions which seemed to be distracting him from experiencing the power of Christ' resurrection, we also need to examine those things which could be destructive to our lives.

What are those 'cherished' things in your lives? Being bitter with a spouse? A friend? A colleague? Or being angry with God? By allowing these emotional issues to remain in us, they can cause us to miss the opportunity to have a meaningful experience with Jesus, the Restorer of the afflicted. Are there any cultural traditions, practices or social connections that are conflicting with your spiritual journey? Am I weakening your capacity to engage in horizontal forgiveness?

It is important to note that such emotional issues can cause us to experience some degree of emotional wounded-ness. Fig 6.2 below illustrates the various degrees of emotional wounded-ness, beginning with damaged, deepest degree of wounded-ness, and gravitating towards the right onto the emotional wholeness.

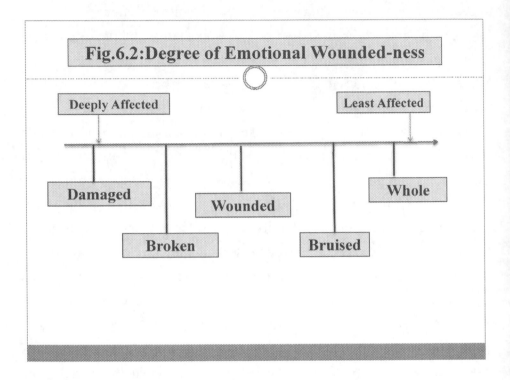

In fact, various situations contribute to the painful emotional 'baggage' which we bring with us. For example, an abusive situation, an unfaithful spouse or a breakdown in a trusting relationship can create emotional baggage. This can emanate from numerous experiences such as living in a dysfunctional family, hypocrisy, mental anguish from a family situation or domestic violence.

In considering the different degrees of emotional wounded-ness, a bruised person is affected slightly. No deep wounds or intense injury exists. Psychologically, there is a dent or impact on the person's feelings, without any brokenness occurring, be it to one's ego, one's emotional stability, one's life or a relationship. Being emotionally wounded suggests that a battle or a fight has occurred, where our defence has been cut, pierced or torn.

Psychologically, by letting down our emotional protection, our feelings become injured. Additionally, a wounded person experiences a high degree of anguish and pain which would require soothing and healing.

When we are broken psychologically, we lose the mental ability to perform our various tasks and a high level of functionality is out of our control. This type of wounded-ness portrays our loss of self-worth, where we perceive ourselves as useless and not as good as others.

> **The desire to examine one's degree of emotional wounded-ness requires open-ness, courage and emotional strength.**

Emotional and psychological damages bring on a degree of harm which affect or impair and reduce our value, usefulness and negatively affect our level of functionality. Furthermore, the traumatic events which we may suffer from, can contribute to our mental instability and to the disfigurement of other aspects of our personhood. In sum, one's degree of emotional wounded-ness, be it being broken or bruised, is measured by the level of functionality which could impact negatively on our healing process.

BOX 6.1: THINKING ANALYTICALLY

M, forty-three year old and J-l, forty year old, are both professionals. They have been experiencing marital difficulties for four years. The couple, parents of three (3) children, on many occasions argued and even have engaged in physical violence. During a bout of physical altercation, J-l informed her husband of her knowledge of his extra-marital relationship. Sessions of blaming and shouting occurred. With the passing of time, Manuel admitted eventually to the deeds. With help from close friends, they signed up for family therapy. After attending a few months of therapy, the couple was helped in becoming aware of the destructive power of the issue. It was then that they acknowledged that they had contributed to the difficulties in the marriage.

The case study above illustrates the consequences of not leaving the past in the past. Furthermore, the negative emotional issues which prevailed in this relationship have contributed to weakening the marital relationship. This couple's situation is typical of how relationships can be affected negatively when painful and difficult issues are not addressed urgently. Actually, leaving the issues for so long signals irresponsibility on the couple's part or indicate that the couple may not have had the emotional and spiritual capacity to address the situation. In particular, it could be that they were driven by the need for power (n Pow), a psychological need which propels individuals to seek to control another person. But there is a notable premise which states that unresolved painful issues do not go away with time, but they only fester and become debilitating. This prolong delay portrays an emotionally unhealthy environment in which they and the children have been residing.

However, these initial therapeutic sessions seemed to have made the positive impact that couples would desire to have for an ailing marriage. Furthermore, various questions come to mind based on the developments in this marriage. Did this couple see the enormity of the issue? Was their marriage relationship beyond reconciliation? The case study in Box 6.1 above provides an example of how issues can hinder a couple's emotional progress. It also illustrates the transformation that can occur when we are willing to bring various suitable resources such as counselling and psychotherapy to bear on our severe difficulties. Through these therapeutic sessions, the married couple and the therapist could discern hindrances, an important step in this stage of the journey *on the road to forgiveness.* Having taken this first step in leaving the past in the past, it would be helpful to continue on the journey by taking the next step.

STEP 2: DISCOVERY OF A CHRIST-CENTRED GOAL

The second step towards leaving the painful past in the past is to discover a Christ-centred goal. In helping to clarify the Apostle Paul's goal, the *Amplified* Bible version explains it this way: "[For my determined purpose is] that I may know Him [that I may progressively become more deeply and intimately acquainted with Him, perceiving and recognizing and understanding the wonders of His Person more strongly and more clearly], and that I may in that same way come to know the power outflowing from His resurrection [which it exerts over believers], and that I may so share His sufferings as to be continually transformed [in spirit into His likeness even] to His death, [in the hope]. That if possible I may attain to the [spiritual and moral] resurrection [that lifts me] out from among the dead [even while in the body]" (Phil 3:10-11). The *New Living Translation* version portrays Paul's goal as follows: "I want to know Christ and experience the mighty power that raised him from the dead. I want to suffer with him, sharing in his death, so that one way or another I will experience the resurrection from the dead!" Having considered these biblical versions of Paul's new desire, the following questions emerge: What was Paul's motivating need? What inspired Paul to respond in this way?

On further analysing the above-mentioned text (Phil 3:10-11), the repetitious use of the word 'knowledge' and its cognates such as 'to know' and 'knowing' denotes an experiential interaction which Paul desired to have with Christ, the Redeemer of the human race. This suggests that Paul was driven by various needs.

First, it seems that he was driven by the need for affiliation (n Aff), which refers to a willingness to set up and maintain social relationships with others. On a spiritual dimension, Paul seemed to have desired spiritual interaction with Christ as an important goal. Charles A. Wanamaker suggests that there was an emphasis between Paul's own identity and his relationship with

Christ.[52] Such a focus is the desired expectation of the Christian believer, where Christ becomes the core of the spiritual relationship.

Second, Paul was driven by the need for intimacy (n Int) on the spiritual dimension. This psychological need creates a desire in individuals to experience warmth and to engage in meaningful relationships. Paul, in seeking to leave the past in the past, focused his energies on various elements of a spiritual relationship with Christ. For example, his goal was not to possess "my own righteousness, which is from the law, but that which is through faith in Christ, the righteousness which is from God by faith" (Phil 3:9). His continuous reference to 'righteousness' confirmed his desire to "conform to the Divine will in purpose, thought and action" which becomes the bedrock for all Divine-human relationships. In supporting the view that the need for intimacy creates an impact, Charles A. Wanamaker further observes that "He [Paul] balances intimate knowledge of Christ … with participation in his suffering."[53] Let us pause at this moment and reflect on a number of searching questions. What would motivate you to leave the past in the past? How willing are you to expend your energies on the positive things of your future? What resources do you need in order to address the painful past issues in your life? What Christ-centred goal are you aiming to achieve?

BOX 6.2: THINKING ANALYTICALLY

As time went on, the therapist was able to lead M and J-l to see the need to forgive each other so that they could move on with their lives and set future plans for their family. However, a few months later, the couple engaged in another heated argument and during that time, J-l reminded M of his former lifestyle outside of their marriage. Being angry and upset, he rushed out of the house and stayed away for a week. In an attempt to cope with his 'ailing' marriage, M began playing golf a few evenings per week. Added to this, he often returned home later than normal in order to avoid the unhealthy state of their relationship.

This couple's situation demonstrates the negative impact of not leaving the painful past in the past. The initial effect of the counselling sessions seemed to have worn off emotionally to the point that they both lost the capacity to sustain the horizontal forgiveness. Furthermore, various questions come to mind based on the developments in this marriage. Did J-l truly forgive her husband? What could have eroded the level of emotional healing that they both had begun to experience? Was their marriage relationship beyond reconciliation? We can conclude that this couple's situation requires divine intervention which should have been included with the counselling sessions. Our capacity to forgive others is divinely-originated and therefore, it is through the power of the Holy Spirit that we can truly leave the painful past in the past.

M's dependence on external factors for peace of mind suggests that he is hiding internal emotional pain. Furthermore, the new interests help to alleviate his stress. However, the impact is not as effective as he hoped, hence the possible reason for him staying away from his home for the prolonged period of time. Moreover, M's focus was on an external locus of happiness and peace which has no guarantee and can be elusive.

On embarking on this step, we see the need to follow the Apostle Paul's determination as captured in the following verse: "No, dear brothers and sisters, I have not achieved it, but I focus on this one thing: Forgetting the past and looking forward to what lies ahead," (Phil 3:13, NLT). Here we see the need to discover our 'one thing', or our solitary pursuit. It is important to ensure that our 'single pursuit' is free to be pursued and is not competing with other interests.

In an attempt to focus on your 'one thing', let's identify some major new Christ-centred goals you would like to accomplish to help you with your emotional and spiritual healing. For example, some of these goals could be to experience freedom from a severe issue or stronghold, to extend forgiveness or be reconciled with someone, or to make peace with an antagonistic

individual Other goals could be to experience emotional healing, to invite
Christ into your life and experience salvation or to confess your wrong-
doings and repent of the injuries you have caused to others. In reflecting
on this aspect of your emotional journey, take some time to identify your
major goals. Let's consider a few things at this time. Do your goals portray
truths about Christ's death? Are your goals uplifting Christ's sacrifice on
Calvary's Cross? Are your goals based on the grace of Christ? Having
considered these questions, select your major goals and write them beside
the arrows in the diagram below:

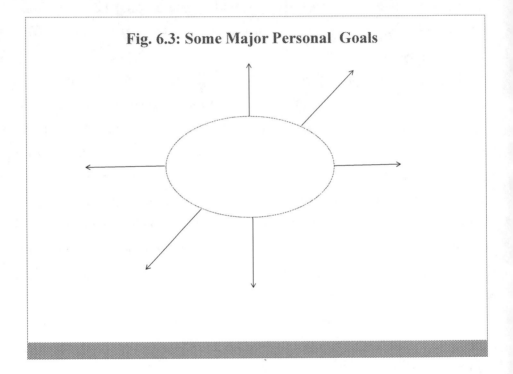

Fig. 6.3: Some Major Personal Goals

Having identified a number of goals, it is important that you zoom in
on one of these and hold it as your 'one thing' or solitary pursuit by placing
it in the centre of the diagram below.

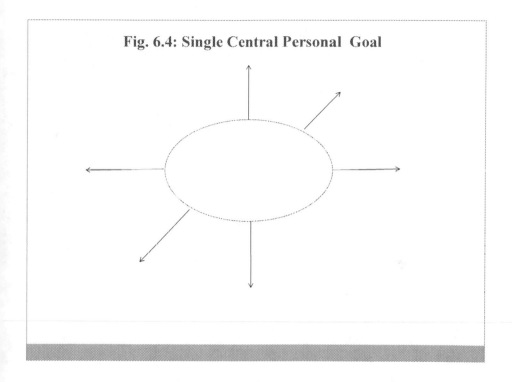

Fig. 6.4: Single Central Personal Goal

Although you have identified your main goal, it is important to be aware that there will be severe competing issues operating against your goal. For instance, the desire to take revenge will surface or there will be a voice ringing in your ears to get 'even' with the perpetrator. It is important to pinpoint these devastating issues by writing them outside the box in the diagram below

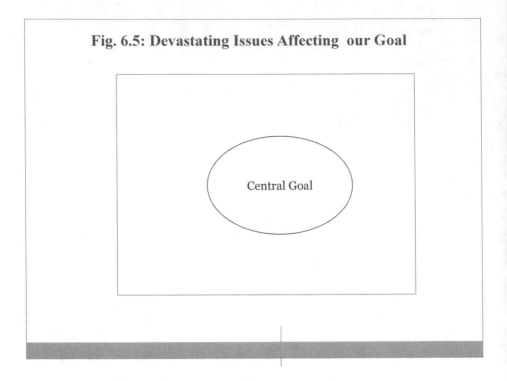

Fig. 6.5: Devastating Issues Affecting our Goal

We have become aware of the competing issues that could impact negatively on your central goal. However, this second step requires you to focus on a Christ-centred goal, hence the need to draw on spiritual resources such as intercessory prayer and fasting to counteract these negative issues. Having worked through step two, it is important to complete this stage of the journey *on the road to forgiveness*, by embarking on step three, which requires you to focus on your new selected Christ-centred goal.

STEP 3: FOCUS ON THE NEW GOAL

The first two steps in this stage have helped us to prepare to leave the past in the past. It is the guiding theme of this chapter. However, we turn to the third step in an attempt to progress on this stage of the journey. In order to focus on our new Christ-centred goal, two sub-goals must be achieved. First, individuals, who eagerly desire to experience emotional progress by focusing on their new Christ-centred goal, need to develop single-mindedness. The *Oxford Dictionary and Thesaurus* define this quality as having one single overriding purpose. To be single-minded signifies having a determined, steadfast and resolute approach to a specific goal. Such a quality requires us to have a sharp narrow focus on our goal and at the same time apply the ability to prevent distractions and competing thoughts from interfering with our main priority. Developing a single-minded attitude also enables us to leave the past in the past and pursue our new Christ-centred goal.

The second sub-goal is to ensure that you do not to live in the past where the destructive emotional issues and your former pain become very visible. By living in the past, we tend to rehearse the injuries we experience and the words which were hurled at us, thereby causing a surge of anger, bitterness and other negative emotions. Such destructive experiences are engineered by the Evil One whose aim is to keep us living in the past.

To avoid living in the past requires that we engage in two processes. Scripture reminds us of these processes: "…forgetting the past and looking forward to what lies ahead" (Phil 3:13, NLT). The first process involves forgetting the past painful issues, the devastating situations and difficult problems that brought about your emotional struggles. The process of forgetting the past involves addressing the situation as has been discussed earlier in this volume. Moreover, it involves turning away from the issue and not mentioning it to your perpetrator. This is an effective method of 'starving' the former painful issue from rising to the surface again. No wonder Scripture advises us to "forget the former things; do not dwell on the past" (Isa 43:18, NIV). Here we envisage the God of Heaven seeking to help us grow emotionally and therefore, you can ask Him to 'flush' your thoughts and mind of the effects of the painful issues and situations.

Meanwhile, the second process involves stretching ourselves beyond the past, the present and seeking to grasp the new direction which Christ has prepared for us. The desire to focus on the future also requires that we take responsibility for our past devastating actions, thereby, providing a conducive atmosphere in which God can play His part. The *New Living Translation* aptly paints the picture this way: "Then if my people who are called by my name will humble themselves and pray and seek my face and turn from their wicked ways, I will hear from heaven and will forgive their sins and restore their land" (2 Chron 7:14). From this scriptural reference, it implies that God desires to take us back to the former difficult issue and to lead us to acknowledge the importance of confession and repentance. On accomplishing this task, the Divine One will lift individuals out of their weakening situation, provide hope and ultimately, ensure emotional restoration.

BOX 6.3: THINKING ANALYTICALLY

They both lived busy lives. J-l was working long hours in her profession and M was attending university during the day and working at night to contribute to the family's finances. A few months later, M and J-l reverted to finger-pointing and rehearsal of past hurtful issues. There was never a week going by without a stormy time in the house. While the children lived through this ordeal, they dare not say a word. They lived in a home where their parents drilled the following words: 'children should be seen but not heard.' The destructive attitudes continued to prevail for months. Even when they summoned various types of help such as psychologists and counsellors, there was no change in their attitude. M continued to play golf more often, using it as a weekend hobby. However, the tense atmosphere at home led him to spend other evenings on the sports field. In the end, M left his home and never returned.

In this example, the couple has regressed emotionally by reverting to their previous destructive behaviours and attitudes. The couple, not being able to cope with the dark side of their relationship, uses this defence mechanism.

Thus, various questions could be asked: Did the therapist take them through all the stages necessary for reconciliation? Did they apply the skills which were taught? Were they sincere about addressing their marital issues?

M's dependence on external factors for peace of mind further suggests that his internal emotional pain was increasing. It confirms that he attributes his peace of mind to golf, an external locus of happiness. Furthermore, the new interests appear to be used to help alleviate his prolonged stress which has originated with the stormy marital relationship. However, the impact from the therapy seemed not to be as effective as he hoped, hence his leaving the matrimonial home.

Since the entire case study in this chapter does not provide any input on the effectiveness of spiritual resources, it would seem that this couple's situation require divine intervention so that the couple can make sense of the situation and gain spiritual support. Indeed, the third step involves accomplishing two sub-goals and engaging in two processes which are essential for leaving the past in the past so that individuals can make progress further with their journey *on the road to forgiveness.*

SUMMARY

In order to leave the past in the past, three steps should be taken. First, pinpoint carefully those areas in your life that could become stronghold by thinking through where you are emotionally and evaluating your emotional health. Furthermore, it is important to examine your level of functionality, through which you can gauge your degree of wounded-ness, be it bruised, broken or damaged. By identifying a Christ-centred goal and focusing on this goal, you would need to develop single-mindedness and apply this quality with the aim of becoming focused on the new goal.

7

FORGIVENESS – A HEALING FACTOR

It was a chilly day when the cold residue from the wintry months lingered on unexpectedly for a few extra days. The theme for the Holy Communion was forgiveness. After the service, Eve, a congregant, approached me with teary eyes and confessed that she was finding it difficult to forgive someone who had offended her. Actually, she further admitted that she did not have the capacity to forgive anyone. During this conversation, she proceeded to alert me that she found it difficult to forgive anyone who hurts her. Visibly, she was dying with an unforgiving spirit from a painful episode between her and another person who had injured her emotionally. Many questions emerge from Eve's experience. Is it necessary to forgive those who have injured us? What benefit does forgiveness provide to our physical and spiritual ill-health? Is everyone able to forgive a perpetrator? In order to address these questions, this chapter examines the Christological view on extending forgiveness to our fellowmen.

From the outset, it is useful to share the principle on which this chapter is based. Nevertheless, let us review this volume's major premise, which states that: *To forgive, a person needs to experience some degree of healing, and to experience healing, an individual needs to forgive herself and others.* (This major principle is illustrated pictorially in Appendix B). With that in mind, we turn to the second portion of this principle as we develop this chapter. So we will focus on the view that in order "… *to experience healing, an individual needs to forgive herself … and others."*

Many individuals bear guilty feelings for various reasons, ranging from lying to murder. People of all walks of life passionately treasure being released from such immoral acts. Such a desire brings us to the place where we should extend forgiveness and experience healing which is the fourth stage of the journey *on the road to forgiveness.*

The inherited sinful disposition of human beings requires that we be forgiven by others and the Divine One. Scripture aptly shares an example of this situation: "When Jesus returned to Capernaum several days later, the news spread quickly that he was back home. Soon the house where he was staying was so packed with visitors that there was no more room, even outside the door. While he was preaching God's word to them, four men arrived carrying a paralyzed man on a mat. They couldn't bring him to Jesus because of the crowd, so they dug a hole through the roof above his head. Then they lowered the man on his mat, right down in front of Jesus. Seeing their faith, Jesus said to the paralyzed man, 'My child, your sins are forgiven.' But some of the teachers of religious law who were sitting there thought to themselves, 'What is he saying? This is blasphemy! Only God can forgive sins!' Jesus knew immediately what they were thinking, so he asked them, 'Why do you question this in your hearts? Is it easier to say to the paralyzed man 'Your sins are forgiven,' or 'Stand up, pick up your mat, and walk?' So I will prove to you that the Son of Man has the authority on earth to forgive sins." Then Jesus turned to the paralyzed man and said, 'Stand up, pick up your mat, and go home!'" (Mk 2:1-11, NLT).

The writer of the second Gospel employs the root word for forgiveness in this passage. Let us examine the term *aphimi* 'to forgive'. It connotes the idea of releasing a person from debt. This word further conveys the idea that the person is permitted to go, to the extent that she is no longer held back by a burden or emotional weight which should have been borne eternally. Thus, forgiveness is the responsibility of the victim to release the perpetrator. To do otherwise, would be to retard ourselves.

BOX 7.1: THINKING ANALYTICALLY

For over a decade, Grandma has not been on speaking terms with her sister, N and N's daughter, P. Initially, this was a very close-knitted family. However, due to old age and sibling rivalry. Grandma and N became distant and their relationship gradually died, thereby creating a ripple effect. Unfortunately, N's children became affected. This was certainly true for P, who was very close to her dear aunt. Although the house visits to Grandma continued by N, there was hardly any conversation. N decided to terminate her visits to her sister since there was no longer a relationship. Furthermore, even though these relatives worshipped regularly at their different denominational churches, the issue was never raised. Later N advised her children not to visit their aunt any longer.

Cases such as this elicit many complex questions. The array of responses indicates that no simple answer can be provided in the next few pages. Some of the questions that come to mind are: What was their level of spirituality? Why did one of the adults not raise the issue? Did they lack the emotional capacity to face the issue? Mark McMinn observes that forgiveness within its theological 'home territory' is captivating and transformative.[54] Failing to address an issue immediately creates difficulties in the medium term and long run when we attempt to face and deal with the painful issues.

To address the second part of the principle on which this chapter is built, namely "*... to experience healing, an individual needs to forgive herself ... and others*", I will examine the following three perspectives: (1) our physical illness is an expression of our inherent spiritual condition; (2) forgiveness leads to restoration and (3) forgiveness engenders freedom.

FIRST PERSPECTIVE: PHYSICAL ILLNESS IS AN EXPRESSION OF OUR INHERENT SPIRITUAL CONDITION

On examining the story in the second chapter of the Gospel of Mark, we could ask the following question: What was the paralytic's most urgent need – relief from his physical sickness or relief from the pain which was caused by his spiritual ill-health? This leads me to ask the central question:

> **Christ responds readily to our quest to escape the icy grip of guilt and shame by providing spiritual healing for our sin-sick soul.**

Why did Jesus, the Healing Messiah, focus on the man's sins and not on his urgent and immediate need, that of physical healing? From the outset, Christ did not ignore the man's physical ailment, but on the contrary, gave it his full attention by dealing with the greater need, that of spiritual healing. Since Jesus' ministry also comprised physical and spiritual healing, it was very unlikely that He would have ignored the physically sick.

Furthermore, physical sickness is derived from spiritual sickness, in that, we became sick because of our sinful nature. The writer of Psalm 51 painted this picture of the spiritual state of human beings by noting that he "… was sinful at birth, sinful from the time my mother conceived me" (Psalm 51; 5, NIV). Although the correction of this spiritual state is beyond our control, it is within the purview of Christ, the Forgiving Redeemer of the world. Additionally, it is important to be aware that "the paralytic found healing for both his soul and body in Christ. He needed health of soul before he could appreciate health of body. Before the physical malady could be healed, Christ must bring relief to the mind, and cleanse the soul from sin. This lesson should not be overlooked. There are today thousands suffering from physical disease who, like the paralytic, are longing for the message, "Thy sins are forgiven." The burden of sin, with its unrest and unsatisfied desires, is the foundation of their maladies. They can find no relief until they come to the Healer of the soul. The peace which He alone can impart would restore vigor [sic] to the mind and health to the body."[55] Thus, Christ does not ignore a plea for physical healing because it is an inner desire of many people today.

I pause at this point to ask a few pertinent questions: How has your innate spiritual condition been impacting on your desire to grow emotionally? What illnesses have you experienced recently? What steps are you taking to develop your relationship with the Creator of the world? What is the connection among the areas of your emotional, physical and psychological wellbeing at present? How aware are you that the inherited spiritual condition of all human beings is the defining issue for all illnesses?

I continue to examine the prevailing view of this section. It is also illustrated by the story of a biblical character who had a congenital disability, in the form of a visual impairment. As Christ walked the dusty terrain of Palestine, the physically disabled man attracted the attention of Jesus' disciples who inquired about the origin of his visual impairment. He must have been groping in his world of darkness. Perhaps, he was positioned strategically near a hallway to beg for money from passers-by. Christ, the Compassionate Saviour, alerted the uncompassionate disciples that the man's blindness had nothing to do with his parents' deeds. In fact, it gave Christ an opportunity to display Yahweh's miraculous power which will bring glory to Him. And so, with divine authority, Christ anointed the eyes of the visually impaired man and sent him to a nearby pool to experience a ceremonial washing.

Similarly, the story of the resurrection of Lazarus, another biblical character, reinforces the view that Christ focuses on the spiritual needs of the sick first. From this story, Lazarus was deteriorating rapidly and was at the point of death. His sisters, Martha and Mary, despatched an urgent message to Jesus, who replied by saying that Lazarus' illness would not result in death, but it would bring glory to Jehovah. His physical need was urgent both to the siblings and to himself. But, based on the development of the story, Lazarus died. Nevertheless, Jesus' divine authority had equipped Him with the power to bring Lazarus back to life. Such miraculous experiences seem to signify that the human race has no place in the cold chilly depths of the earth, but that we were made to live in an everlasting state. Just as Christ zoomed in on the spiritual dimension of Lazarus, he also did likewise to the paralytic man by extending forgiveness for his sins. This was an indication that he has the desire and ability "to make the presence of the awaited kingdom felt in tangible ways."[56] So like Lazarus, it is possible for our physical healing to emerge from our spiritual healing. As we continue with this journey *on the road to forgiveness,* our quest for wholeness brings us closer to the Omnipotent One, who is willing to extend unconditional forgiveness, which is a healing factor.

BOX 7.2: THINKING ANALYTICALLY

Sometime later, as N and her children attended a religious service one weekend, they were greeted with a sermon which encouraged people to forgive each other. After spending some time in prayer, N and her daughter, P, gained the courage and had developed the emotional capacity to discuss the issue with Grandma. It took at least three (3) weeks before Grandma could come to terms with facing the issue herself. Almost every week, N's church attendance was greeted with messages about addressing the painful past issues in one's life. N and her family continued to attend the religious services on a weekly basis.

Pause with me here to examine this case study. This case demonstrates that our tendency to hurt is derived from inherent sin. Moreover, it reveals the positive impact that spiritual resources can have on our emotional difficulties. Psychologically, it appears that Grandma was stuck and therefore, was unable to move forward. This could be the reason she was unable to face the issue during the discussion. It may have been useful if the family in this case had attended some form of counselling session, be it psychotherapy or pastoral counselling.

Importantly, church attendance and prayer are two religious practices which religious people use as coping strategies. These resources indicate that there is a place for religion in the life of emotionally-distressed individuals. Nevertheless, these religious practices only become effective in developing positive emotional wellbeing when we give attention to the act of forgiveness. Actually, when we engage in a life of prayer, the Divine Spirit inspires us to reflect inwardly in order to identify undesirable attitudes and behaviours. Since unforgiving thoughts lead to negative emotions such as anger and bitterness, it is essential to internalise the processes leading to horizontal forgiveness and apply them to our lives, which can bring about a level of restoration.

SECOND PERSPECTIVE: FORGIVENESS LEADS TO RESTORATION

The restoration of people with disabilities to a life of normality is prevalent in Jesus' healing ministry in the Gospel of Mark. The display of this ministry is seen in Christ's extension of this type of pastoral care to the man with a withered hand (Mk 3:1-6). Other examples of this type of care are seen in: (1) the restoration of senses to the individual with a hearing and speech impediment (Mk 7:31-37); (2) the restoration of sight to a resident of Bethsaida who was visually impaired (Mk8:22-26); and (3) the provision of emotional and mental stability to the boy with epilepsy (Mk 9:14-29). These examples identify the various contexts in which the divine healing power is displayed, thus bringing about restoration on different levels.

Furthermore, healing is also evident in Mk 2:1-12, where an attitude of forgiveness is conveyed to a man with paralysis. This biblical account conveys the theme of paralysis which is defined as the relaxing of the nerves of one's side. Let us examine this idea closer. A major concern emerges immediately: Is he a paraplegic, quadriplegic or hemiplegic? Does he have global paralysis? Medically, paralysis is the loss of muscle formation and feelings in the affected areas. It is also caused by damage to the nervous system, mainly the spinal cord. Also, strokes and traumatic situations can cause paralysis. Such physical conditions can have implications for our holistic restoration.

Although there may be a link between the man's physical healing and the type of paralysis he had, there was a spiritual connection. The character in this episode had contracted paralysis of the entire soul from birth, hence the reason Jesus focused primarily on the forgiveness of his sins. Christ's attitude towards the paralytic

Although Christ showed compassion to the weak and hurting, His ultimate focus is on restoring the human race to its rightful spiritual state with the Divine Creator.

man and his handling of the situation in the story indicate that we are not necessarily sick because we have sinned, but because of sin, we are subject to the effects of sin, one of which is paralysis of the body. The focus on his sinful condition, therefore, demonstrates that forgiveness leads to spiritual restoration, whereby, an individual can reconnect with the Creator of the universe.

Furthermore, it is true that during the time spanning from Aaron to Jesus' era, it was the prerogative of the priests to speak and act on behalf of God, and to declare sinners free of illnesses. However, with Jesus extending forgiveness to the paralytic man, it created a theological dispute between himself and the religious rulers of his day, to the point that the religious leaders accused Christ of equating himself with God. However, since he took on the role of intercessor in the heavenly sanctuary for all humanity, a role similar to that of the High Priest, it is therefore within his divine right to extend forgiveness to hurting individuals. N. T. Wright pinpoints the powerful nature of forgiveness and observes that when individuals engage in forgiveness, the impact reaches to the core of one's personality, thereby, assisting with the healing of past obscured hurts.[57] Since Jesus and the Father are one, and it is God, who is offended every time we engage in sinful behaviours, then Jesus, who is God, has the authority to extend forgiveness, thereby, restoring us spiritually.

Second, Jesus seeks to restore individuals on the physical level as seen in the discourse between the paralytic man and Himself. Scripture provides a terse account: "I say to you, arise, pick up *and* carry your sleeping pad *or* mat, and be going on home. And he arose at once and picked up the sleeping pad *or* mat and went out before them all, so that they were all amazed and recognized *and* praised *and* thanked God, saying, We have never seen anything like this before!" (Mk 2:11-12, AMP). Although the man's quest for physical healing was paramount to him, it became secondary in the divine scheme of events.

We are reminded that "in the healing of the paralytic at Capernaum, Christ again taught the same truth. It was to manifest His power to forgive sins that the miracle was performed. And the healing of the paralytic also illustrates other precious truths. It is full of hope and encouragement, and from its connection with the [*fault-finding*] Pharisees it has a lesson of warning as well. Like the leper, this paralytic had lost all hope of recovery. His disease was the result of a life of sin, and his sufferings were embittered by remorse. He had long before appealed to the Pharisees and doctors, hoping for relief from mental suffering and physical pain."[58] Such a situation explains the reason for the second tension which existed between Jesus and the many religious leaders. On the one hand, Christ, the Compassionate

Healer was working to relief helpless and suffering individuals, while these leaders were criticising his actions.

Third, individuals who receive forgiveness tend to experience social restoration, to the extent, that they are able to reunite with their community. The paralytic man was on the margin of his community, and by extension, on the periphery of society because of his illness.

Ellen G. white insightfully remarked that the Pharisees "coldly pronounced him incurable, and abandoned him to the wrath of God. The Pharisees regarded affliction as an evidence of divine displeasure, and they held themselves aloof from the sick and the needy. Yet often these very ones who exalted themselves as holy were more guilty than the sufferers they condemned."[59] The corresponding event in the Gospel of St Matthew echoed that the healed man went to his house, suggesting that he also was restored to the members of his household.

BOX 7.3: THINKING ANALYTICALLY
It was about a year after the initial effort to address the situation that Grandma took sick and had to be hospitalised. P remarked to her mother that she believed the time was right for them to discuss the matter fully with her aunt. The three occasions Grandma spent in hospital allowed her to focus on her spirituality, thus, giving her and N the opportunity to face the issues. P and her mum were determined to address the situation since the aunt's health was deteriorating. It took three sessions to pinpoint the problem and admit their errors, the unwholesome behaviour and attitude that were displayed to each other. Three months later, N was attending his sister's funeral with ambivalence.

Take some time now to consider this aspect of the case. In providing an analysis of the case, the length of time which Grandma took to face the situation seems to confirm that she was stuck psychologically. Furthermore, it appears that she did not possess the emotional capacity to either forgive her sister and niece or to request an apology. Taking a look at the issue of Grandma's health, it could be her failing health that engineered the willingness on her part to face up to the situation. Individuals crave for peace of mind and freedom from guilt and shame. By extending forgiveness to her relatives, Grandma was paving the way for the relationship to be revived and be restored among herself, N and her children. Although it was a sad occasion when Grandma passed away, N's family would have been elated that they had reconciled with her.

Individuals who embark on the journey towards forgiveness can experience a level of restoration, whereby they can feel a part of the community, the ethnic group or the family one more time. More importantly, complete healing occurs when an individual is restored, be it to his former activities in life, to the community, his family or workplace. In moving onto the third perspective, I pause to pose the following questions: Have you been ostracised because of an emotional injury you have caused a family member, fellow church member or friend? What are your relationships like? Are you stuck emotionally because you are unable to engage in horizontal forgiveness? Or do you lack the capacity to forgive others?

THIRD PERSPECTIVE: FORGIVENESS ENGENDERS FREEDOM

In extending forgiveness to others, we experience freedom. Importantly, we enjoy freedom from the prolonged emotional, physical and spiritual consequences of the sinful attitude we may have been carrying for a while. We gain freedom from disgrace, guilt and shame. We become free so that we are able to walk the corridors of our school, university or workplace again. It affords us the freedom to walk the streets without looking over our shoulders. Interpersonal forgiveness imparts the freedom to live in our own home and interact meaningfully with members of our household once more. When we forgive others, there is freedom again to engage in the life of our denominational place of worship. Emerging from this new experience is the opportunity to worship the Divine One freely because no condemnation exists in our heart.

Additionally, when we engage in horizontal forgiveness, we are no longer held back, held down or held up at the emotional, psychological or spiritual level. As the Greek word *aphiemi* 'to forgive' suggests, we are released from the emotional burden of negativity. Having reached this stage, we no longer remain a slave to that painful issue which has been creating unforgiving thoughts or driving us to display undesirable attitudes. Since forgiveness is a healing factor, by extending horizontal forgiveness to others, we can embark on the next journey as we progress towards total wholeness.

The willingness to extend forgiveness remind me of a four-year old story across the Atlantic. Early that year a bewildered young man walked into a police station and told the officer on duty to arrest him because he had just shot his fiancée in her head. He had shot the young lady who was his girlfriend for three years. They had been arguing for thirty-eight hours, a heated discussion which culminated when the young man shot the girl in her face. Four days later when her condition did not improve, her parents removed the life support from her.

As the daughter lay in the ICU, her father heard the following words vibrating in his mind: "forgive him." He felt it was impossible to do so. Later, as he prayed in his room, he recognised that not only would his daughter want him to extend forgiveness, but it is a divine imperative. Although the family agreed to extend forgiveness, the prosecutor was extremely sceptical. Biblical forgiveness is pardon, choosing not to punish. There are times when such a decision, while difficult, is not complicated. This is not such a situation. In fact, the family's decision to extend forgiveness to the young man would enable him to redeem his crime after he leaves prison in a way he could not if he were there for life. For instance, he indicated that he will be volunteering in animal shelters because of his former girlfriend's love for animals. Similar renewed spiritual states contributes to our willingness to fellowship with others, Knowing that we have been set free, adds value to the fact that we have taken the journey *on the road to forgiveness.*

The freedom derived from forgiveness extends to joy. The writer of Psalm 51 yearned for this experience, thus he bore his soul to the God of Heaven:

> Purge me with hyssop, and I shall be clean;
>> Wash me, and I shall be whiter than snow.
> Make me hear joy and gladness,
>> *That* the bones You have broken may rejoice.
> Hide Your face from my sins,
>> And blot out all my iniquities.
> Create in me a clean heart, O God,
>> And renew a steadfast spirit within me.
> Do not cast me away from Your presence,
>> And do not take Your Holy Spirit from me.
> Restore to me the joy of Your salvation,
>> And uphold me *by Your* generous Spirit.

 (Psalm 51:7-12).

This portion of the Psalm is littered with words such as 'purge', 'wash' and 'blot out', which relates to the idea of cleansing. So when we are forgiven, it creates an image that the deed has been washed thoroughly. Within the context of this portion of the Psalm, the writer desires to 'rejoice' and craves for both 'joy and gladness' and 'the joy of … salvation'. From this, we observe that the writer's desire for joy emerges because forgiveness creates freedom. And when we are free, there is elation, joy and jubilation in our hearts. Certainly forgiveness is a healing factor for our emotional, physical, psychological and spiritual wounds!

Such perspectives help us to grasp another lesson from the episode involving the paralytic man. Based on the interaction among the major characters in the story, it is evident that forgiveness and healing are interdependent. More importantly, the theological principle is that forgiveness is central to our healing on various levels. This is based on the view that "there are today thousands suffering from physical disease, who like the paralytic, are longing for the message, 'Thy sins are forgiven.' The burden of sin, with its unrest and unsatisfied desires, is the foundation of their maladies. They can find no relief until they come to the Healer of the soul. The peace which He alone can give, would impart vigor [sic] to the mind, and health to the body."[60] The inherent nature of sin brings about disease, whose healing is beyond our control, hence the need to turn to Jesus, the Compassionate and Redeeming Healer of the sick.

Furthermore, there is an explicit connection between healing and forgiveness. When we extend horizontal forgiveness to others, there is always healing for the soul, even though healing for the body may not be gained. I reflectively ask: When was the last time you had to forgive someone? What impact did it have on you? What motivated you to extend forgiveness? Based on the above views, forgiveness is critical to healing beyond the physical realm, thereby indicating that forgiveness is a healing factor.

Victor D. Marshall

SUMMARY

In the beginning, this chapter set out to answer three questions: Is it necessary to forgive those who have injured us? What benefit does forgiveness provide to our emotional, physical and spiritual ill-health? Is everyone able to forgive a perpetrator? Furthermore, the chapter is based on the principle which indicates that "… to experience healing, an individual needs to forgive themselves … and others." A perspective which emerges is that our physical illness has its foundation in the human's inherent spiritual illness. Additionally, forgiveness affords individuals the opportunity to be restored on at least three levels: physical, social and spiritual. Ultimately, forgiveness contributes to experiencing freedom from negative emotions. Hence, we can agree that forgiveness is a healing factor.

8

PSYCHOLOGICAL BENEFITS
OF FORGIVENESS

A rich, famous, powerful political individual had asked a few trusted business consultants to manage the huge finances of his growing and prosperous private business. The team of consultants consisted of a senior consultant, a junior partner and a trainee. Since he was very busy with his political portfolio, he lacked the time to give any valuable attention to the state of his financial empire. Nevertheless, the well-qualified consultants worked tirelessly and on odd hours to ensure that the business flourished. They identified creative avenues that would generate huge finances. Along with this financial venture, they sharply curtailed huge expenditure. Their instructions were to spend as little as possible and to make as much money as was possible. And in response, they followed the advice to the letter, so it seemed.

After secretly securing a few days away from the pressured political portfolio, the rich business owner speedily summoned his consultants to update him on the state of his finances. Rumours of all type had been polluting the business environment and offensively circulating the office, until eventually they reached the busy and secretive business owner. In fact, he decided to settle his financial records by examining the receipt books and other financial records with his consultants.

On starting to examine the financial reports, the business owner recognised that a client had owed him thousands of British pound sterling. A few days later the senior consultant informed the indebted client that he needed to meet with his creditor to settle his financial commitment. Unfortunately, he had other huge financial debts hovering over his head. This meant that he was not in a good financial position. Since he could not pay his creditor, the rich powerful business owner confiscated his few possessions and ordered the poor client and his family to work for him without pay until the huge debt was repaid.

But the distressed client desperately fell on his knees and passionately begged him to be patient with him and give him some time to get his finances in order so that he can repay the entire debt. The businessman contemplated on the client's sentiments. On being moved with compassion, he changed his plans and forgave his client and cancelled all of his debts.

How do we feel when we forgive others? What happens to us when we are forgiven? Such questions guide this chapter which focuses on inter- and intra-personal issues in relation to the psychological benefits of horizontal forgiveness. In order to address these questions, this chapter deals with (1) the regulation of negative emotions, (2) fulfilment of psychological needs and (3) pro-social psychological changes.

REGULATION OF NEGATIVE EMOTIONS

Individuals who work towards developing the capacity to forgive others often contribute positively to the regulation of negative emotions in their lives. In order to develop the capacity to engage in horizontal forgiveness, it is important for individuals to re-appraise their attitude and behaviour towards the people who may have hurt them.

Adjusting their internal views and addressing their emotional pain are processes which assist hurting people in dealing with psychological ailments such as anger, anxiety, depression, and hostility. Nevertheless, such negative emotions can be classified, with anxiety and depression

> **A spirit of unforgiveness can create a number of psychological drawbacks which result in individuals experiencing low moods and displaying ill-feelings towards others.**

being identified as negative moods, while anger and hostility are termed as negative feelings.

When we reflect on the impact of these negative emotions, we would agree that "the relation that exists between the mind and the body is very intimate. When one is affected, the other sympathizes. The condition of the mind affects the health to a far greater degree than many realize. Many of the diseases from which men suffer are the result of mental depression. Grief, anxiety, discontent, remorse, guilt, distrust, all tend to break down the life forces and to invite decay and death. Disease is sometimes produced, and is often greatly aggravated, by the imagination. Many are lifelong invalids who might be well if they only thought so. Many imagine that every slight exposure will cause illness, and the evil effect is produced because it is expected. Many die from disease the cause of which is wholly imaginary. Courage, hope, faith, sympathy, love promote health and prolong life. A contented mind, a cheerful spirit, is health to the body and strength to the soul. In the treatment of the sick the effect of mental influence should not be overlooked. Rightly used, this influence affords one of the most effective agencies for combating disease."[61] The connection between extending forgiveness to others and the existence of positive emotions in our lives indicates that there is a direct relationship between these two variables. Hence, in order to counteract

> ### BOX 8.1: THINKING ANALYTICALLY
>
> Ms D, who is about forty years old, has been experiencing low moods, guilt due to her undesirable behaviour and distrust which had developed from a number of intimate relationships which had terminated abruptly. After the trust in the therapeutic relationship had been achieved during a series of supporting therapy sessions, involving spiritual disciplines such as prayer, she admitted that she felt as though she had been 'taken for a ride' during the various intimate relationships. She shared that while the relationships had promises of being long-lasting, such a situation never materialised. She has become angry and hostile. Also, she has been having sleepless nights and has lost her self-confidence. Moreover, she has lost interest in developing other intimate relationships because she is still angry and she also believes all of them would end in the same manner.

these life-weakening forces, it seems essential for emotionally-hurting people and perpetrators to engage in horizontal forgiveness.

Ms D's case is an example of what various therapists encounter when working with clients. Should she develop similar attitudes to all male companions based on her previous experiences? Should she be encouraged to be angry? Is she emotionally prepared for another intimate relationship at the moment? Should she make her feelings known to her former male fiancés, if they are available? Such complex questions seem necessary in relation to the idea of extending horizontal forgiveness.

Ms D's negative emotional feelings of anger and hostility seem understandable, although not justifiable. Individuals, who endeavour to progress successfully with their lives, also need positive emotional health. One's emotional well-being is critical to amicable interaction with others and to the resolution of emotional difficulties. Furthermore, as individuals seek to advance in their studies or in their careers, it would be important for them to begin to experience emotional maturity.

It seems clear that various elements, such as mistrust and anger are preventing Ms Danger from taking the journey *on the road to forgiveness*, during which time she would be able to pass through the various stages. Additionally, by holding stereotypical views of her previous male fiancés, this situation could have been preventing Ms D from extending horizontal forgiveness. Admittedly, negative stereotypical behaviours blur our vision and prevent us from gaining a clear perspective of the situations around us. By holding a negative stereotypical view, we perceive everyone we encounter in the same manner and therefore, find it difficult to alter our view of them. In fact, this type of attitude negatively impacts our interactions with others and therefore makes social relationships more difficult to form.

When we consider Ms D's stereotypical attitude, we could conclude that anger, which emerges from unresolved emotional issues, contributes to individuals becoming psychologically fixated. She is experiencing the emotional stuck syndrome in relation to intimate relationships. It is noticeable that emotional progress becomes difficult to achieve when horizontal forgiveness is withheld. Thus, this case leads us to ponder on various personal questions: What is holding you back from forgiving the person who hurt you? With what emotional issues are you stuck? How intense is the anger you are carrying presently? Can you honestly say that you can forgive your perpetrator wholeheartedly?

Scripture counsels us on how to deal with anger as a negative emotion: "But now put away *and* rid yourselves [completely] of all these things: anger, rage, bad feeling toward others, curses *and* slander, and foulmouthed abuse *and* shameful utterances from your lips!" (Col 3:8, AMP). Among these unwholesome, immoral attitudes and vice are a number of negative feelings namely anger, rage and bad feelings towards others. The Greek word *orge* 'anger' denotes an impulsive violent feeling emerging from within us. The *Amplified Bible* version depicts the intensity with which anger bears down on the victim, by noting that "a hot-tempered man stirs up strife, but he who is slow to anger appeases contention" (Prov 15:18, AMP). Since anger is a destructive feeling, we are encouraged to discard these negative emotions like unwanted clothing. One way by which this can be achieved is by embarking on the journey of horizontal forgiveness. Such a process contributes to one's emotional maturity, thus a pre-requisite for meeting psychological needs.

FULFILMENT OF PSYCHOLOGICAL NEEDS

Individuals are motivated in life on the account of a number of in-born, natural and spontaneous needs such as food, security and love. In fact, these relate to people's aesthetic, emotional, physiological and psychological needs which must be fulfilled in order for them to grow and develop.[62] In focusing on people's psychological needs, I hold the view that extending horizontal forgiveness is beneficial to the fulfilment of these psychological needs. In particular, this section examines two areas of our lives to which forgiveness are beneficial: the fulfilment of a sense of belonging and maintaining one's self esteem.

Maslow (1943) noted that individuals, who successfully meet their basic needs such as food, sleep and warmth, soon become focused on fulfilling higher order motivational needs, such as esteem and seeking personal growth. One of the higher order needs is the belonging needs, which refer to a desire to be loved by others and also to love others. Individuals, who are concerned with achieving these needs, have a desire for strong interpersonal relationships with others such as family members and friends among others. Along with this innate desire is also the need to display love and affection. With this in mind, I am instigated to pose the following questions: Do you feel loved? What does your circle of friendship look like? What is your interaction with others like? With whom do you display mutual affection? With whom do you have similar interests? Most of the time, what emerges from within you emotionally- anger, hatred or love?

Importantly, these types of familial and social relationships are founded on unmerited love which is filled profoundly with positive emotions and sentiments towards family members, friends and relatives among others. However, in the event that the need for belonging is unmet, individuals become,,,

… psychologically dysfunctional. This disorder occurs in the form of anger and hostility among other psychological problems to the point that there is behavioural, cognitive or emotional distress.

These aspects of distress bring about a breakdown on any of these three levels, hence referring to this phenomenon as a psychological dysfunction.[63] A factor which can contribute to this is an unforgiving attitude or a lack of apologies. Psychological researchers such as Aaron Lazare conclude that receiving an apology helps the victim, whereby some of their psychological need are met.[64] Such an explanation could be a major reason for emotionally-injured individuals being emotionally stuck and unable to progress emotionally.

Forming negative thoughts of others; exhibiting hatred and bitterness; and displaying negative stereotypical attitudes are examples of poor behavioural, cognitive and emotional functioning.

Another aspect of the belonging needs is the need to love. Individuals also are driven to display affection and compassion to friends. This inner human psychological desire reminds me of an ancient story involving the biblical King David, a Judean, and Shimei, who was a member of the Israelite tribe of Benjamin. This Benjamite had begrudged the newly-crowned monarch because he had been chosen to replace the former King who was a very popular Benjamite. On seeing the King approaching the community, Shimei immediately began to disrespect the new King by hurling swear words at him. This was not the only discourteous act he performed. He also threw stones at the king and all the king's officials who were accompanying him on his royal trip. And it was not a one-off incident. Shimei stalked the king. Every time King David stepped forward courageously to continue his journey, Shimei swore at him. It was a constant battle. The atmosphere must have been filled with tension. The attacker was aggressive. And to 'add salt to the wounds', he continued to hurl stones at him and rained dirt on the king. You could imagine how dusty the king's clothes had looked. Did the dust settle? Would he kill the king eventually? The biblical account is silent on these issues. Nevertheless, the attack was ongoing. It must have felt like eternity. This treatment towards the king must have been embarrassing for him.

Along with the swearing, Shimei verbally attacked the king, referring to him as a murderer and a scoundrel. Prophetically, he proclaimed assumingly that divine punishment had come to the king's doorstep, and that was the reason for the problems in his home. With this Benjamite inflicting emotional pain on the king, one of his officials passionately sought permission to behead Shimei. But the king stepped forward to quell a possible murder. Soon after, the king comforted himself by acknowledging that divine providence was involved. During that gruelling experience, the ancient king became exhausted. But soon after, he refreshed himself.

Time had elapsed. The king had transacted his business. And now he was returning to his homeland. But he had only reached as far as the Jordan, the western neighbour of ancient Judah, when his countrymen had come out to meet him and to escort him across the Jordan River belt. And then out of the 'blue', Shimei, the Benjamite, emerged from obscurity, and hurried down with the men of Judah to meet King David. A thousand other Benjamites had accompanied him, along with Ziba, the steward of Saul's household, and his fifteen sons and twenty servants. It was a frantic atmosphere. Everyone rushed hurriedly to the Jordan, where the king was located. Then they crossed over to be at the king's service with whatever chores he had asked to be done. It was a changed scene.

Without much fanfare or noise, Shimei crossed over, fell outstretched on the ground at the king's feet and then confessed. He then surprisingly admitted that he had made some mistakes. He had hurt the King. He openly admitted that he was guilty. And he recalled, in detail, his unsightly deeds to him. It was as though the internal guilt was gnawing at his consciences. He catalogued his woeful behaviour to the king as though King David had not known. Some things seem hard to forgive. And so Abishai, one of the king's officials suggested that Shimei should be executed for ill-treating the king. Well, as he put it, Shimei had cursed the LORD's anointed and therefore, did not deserve to live. But King David would have none of it. He seemed to recognise that every human being has an inner drive to express love, particularly to their enemies and perpetrators. So he intercepted and for the second time, quenched a potential cold-blooded killing. King David refused to entertain an angry disposition or even endorse a hostile and revengeful attitude. The king was forceful, emphatic and forgiving. His questions signalled his intentions - Should anyone be put to death today? Don't I know that today I am king over Israel?" And then he offered a regal pardon to Shimei and assured him that he was forgiven. This drama is an example of the perspective that when individuals express love towards others, it enables them to forgive. In fact, the barriers of anger, hostility and un-forgiveness prevent individuals from fulfilling the need for love.

The second facet of our life which benefits from the act of forgiving is the maintenance of our self-esteem. Individuals who forgive others create an impact on their self-esteem, in that, such individuals regain their confidence. This erases any fear they may have of their opponents. The author of the biblical book of Romans corroborates this perspective by assuring us that "there is no condemnation for those who belong to Christ Jesus" (Rom 8:1, NLT). The *New King James* version expanded this theological thought by explaining that "there is therefore now no condemnation to those who are in Christ Jesus, who do not walk according to the flesh, but according to the Spirit." This development is how the act of forgiveness contributes to our emotional progress. By engaging in spiritual processes such as confessing and experiencing salvation, individuals tend to progress with their journey *on the road to forgiveness.*

What stage of the journey on the road to forgiveness are you at, after having read this portion of the chapter? How did you respond when you were tempted to adopt an unforgiving attitude? Another impact which forgiveness has on people's self-esteem is that it inspires people to respect others and demonstrate an attitude that they can trust others. And when we regain our self-esteem, we are less threatened by emotional hurts and our self-esteem become more stable. Maintaining one's self-esteem is an indication that individuals who regain their self-esteem are on their way to having their higher order needs to be met. This affords such individuals to develop emotionally and psychologically. Individuals who have these set of needs met tend to engage in long-lasting and meaningful relationships. But how does forgiveness contribute psychologically to social relationships is the focus of the next section.

PRO-SOCIAL PSYCHOLOGICAL CHANGES

Individuals, who extend horizontal forgiveness to others within the context of a relationship, contribute to emotional progress along the hierarchy of holistic restoration healing model. One psychological benefit is that forgiveness promotes harmony in relationships among others. Achieving such harmonious relationships come about through the journey towards reconciliation and the recovery step as is seen in Fig. 8.1 below. However, prior to undergoing the journey towards reconciliation, individuals who engage in horizontal forgiveness would also need to embark on a journey towards freedom.

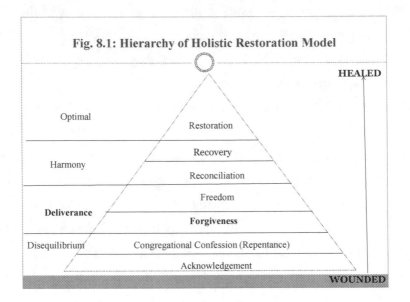

Fig. 8.1: Hierarchy of Holistic Restoration Model

At the outset, individuals who engage in horizontal forgiveness go through the deliverance phase which involves addressing the painful issues by surrendering them to Christ, the Healing Saviour, and also by leaving the past in past. On progressing up the hierarchy, individuals also need to experience freedom in order to be delivered emotionally from the painful issues. This second journey on the hierarchy involves breaking the emotional stronghold through intercessory prayer and fasting; and detoxing your emotional self of the pain and negative emotions. Furthermore, on becoming delivered, it is important to speak life into your being. Additionally, to gain emotional freedom requires you to unwrap the layers of your painful past. This could involve getting rid of unfavourable thoughts such as suicidal tendencies and the 'good-for-nothing' sentiments uttered by others. By peeling off these layers which have produced negativity in your life, you experience a transformation which brings about your deliverance.

Having experienced emotional deliverance, it is essential for individuals to take the journey towards reconciliation. From the hierarchy of holistic restoration model, this emotional journey involves various stages such as acknowledging that a problem has existed between the victim and his/her perpetrator. To acknowledge or admit that a painful issue has occurred requires honest, soul-searching and thoughtful reflection. To generate truth and reality suggests that individuals must draw out painful memories and uncomfortable thoughts from the deep recesses of one's life. Added to this stage, is the view that conflicts and emotional hurts bring consequences. To progress, individuals should accept these inevitable consequences, an action which can be helpful to the healing process.

Empirical research reveals that reconciliation consists of psychological components such as closeness and trust.[65] However, closeness denotes being near to someone in a relationship; bounded by similar interests and affections. On a deeper level, closeness brings about warmth, which could only exist if anger and hostility are absent. In order for the relationship between individuals to be reconciled, the social or familial relationship must be repaired, thereby enabling emotional healing to take place. This process is another stage in this journey. And if it is not allowed to take place, the journey of reconciliation would be halted.

Added to this particular journey on the hierarchy of holistic restoration is the step of recovery, which makes up the harmony phase on the restoration model. The recovery step involves a 'settling down' of the reconciled relationship, whereby the previously injured individuals can regain their emotional balance between them. In this phase, values such as trust and confidentiality are addressed, while qualities such as love and kindness begin to be exhibited again. Individuals who experience healing on any level also begin to re-engage with others socially or intimately as long as it is safe and appropriate. Such actions and attitudes contribute to the harmony in relationships, thereby assisting individuals' degree of healing to rise higher towards the optimal phase. Have you recovered from your emotional difficulty to the point of experiencing some degree of healing? Have you settled down emotionally from the issue? Have you recuperated from the after-effects of emotional pain which you have suffered?

SUMMARY

Intentional and meaningful steps to repair relationships bring about a measure of benefits. This chapter examined the psychological benefits which could be derived from extending horizontal forgiveness. One benefit is that forgiveness assists with the regulation of negative emotions such as anger, hatred and hostility. Furthermore individuals who extend forgiveness to others contribute to their higher order needs being met. The need to belong and be loved along with the fulfilment of self-esteem needs can be achieved through the act of forgiveness. Failure to meet these needs tends to result in individuals becoming psychologically dysfunctional. A third benefit is that familial and social relationships regain harmony, thereby bringing about closeness, trust and warmth between individuals.

9

EXPERIENCING EMOTIONAL
AND SPIRITUAL HEALING

At some point in our life we have been subjected to injustice in one form or the other. Injustice appears in various shades – angry outburst, false accusations, hatred and insults to name a few. Although such events can bring prolonged emotional pain and burning anguish, some individuals who eagerly desire to move on with their life, extend forgiveness to the perpetrator and seek help through attending therapeutic and counselling sessions. Some of us have been unable to locate our perpetrators. Nevertheless, mentally, we have extended forgiveness by releasing them from our minds and ceasing to hold any raging revengeful attitude. We regain the capacity to progress emotionally and function well again in the various sphere of our life.

An example of such experiences is carved in an episode of the dramatic twist of events in the life of the biblical character, Joseph, a seventeen-year old Jewish lad, whose mother had passed away. This almost tragic story features the young lad living in Canaan with his father, his sister and eleven male siblings. On one occasion when he accompanied his brothers in the fields to feed his father's flock, it appeared that he had observed some form of misbehaviour among them. In his jubilant and exciting youthful age, this teenager engineered a hurtful, displeasing and painful report of his brothers and anxiously shared it with his father. It was heart-wrenching for the older boys. Later, as divine providence would have it, this innocent and jovial youth dreamt that he would be in charge of the entire family. To be specific, he informed them that all of them would have to bow down to him. With him being his father's favourite son, a product of a dysfunctional family in which favouritism has been prevalent for three generations, the unwelcomed news angered and enraged everyone.

Sometime later, Jacob, the father, despatched Joseph with packages of lunch for his sons who were caring for his flock in the fields. It was an uncalculated and risky decision which Jacob made. Soon after, it ripped his heart into pieces. Immediately, Joseph was placed in the spotlight. To prove that he had loved him greatly, Jacob made a long-sleeved, multi-coloured coat for Joseph. On spotting Joseph approaching them, the anger-infested, brutal, heartless and uncaring brothers immediately thought of exterminating him totally. We come face to face with the chilling, but inspiring perspective that "no thought of the long journey he had made to meet them, of his weariness and hunger, of his claims upon their hospitality and brotherly love, softened the bitterness of their hatred. The sight of the coat, the token of their father's love [for Joseph] filled them with frenzy."[66] Nevertheless, after intensively debating about killing Joseph, the brothers spared his life and simply dumped him into a deep, empty well.

The writer reveals the significance of the impact of this traumatic experience on Joseph's life by using the technique of contrast between love and hatred. The repetitive use of love and hatred indicates the tension which prevailed between Joseph and his brothers and by extension, in this family.[67] Emotions ran high in the hearts of these marginalised brothers. The hatred in their hearts intensified and was transformed into a jealous anger, leading to envy. The brothers, being possessed with such ardent feelings, seemed to have been overcome with an intense desire to annihilate the dreamer. But instead of letting him suffer indefinitely and inhumanely in the well, they sold him to a group of merchants. Then life took another twist when he was sold as a slave to an Egyptian. It was the unexpected. This was an unimaginable experience in the life of a Hebrew national. To be sold as a slave was degrading and humiliating.

In reflecting on Joseph's journey, we wonder what drove the infuriated brothers to mistreat him. And to add 'salt to the

> **The need for affiliation (n Aff) is a psychological need that motivates individuals to have a desire to belong to a group and also have a desire to be liked by others.**

wound', they deceived Jacob by bringing home Joseph's blood-soaked, multi-coloured coat and suggested to their father that Joseph had been devoured by a ferocious animal. Psychologically, the brothers seemed to have been ignored, isolated and marginalised. They seemed to have lost their place in their father's eyes. The only solution they could think of was to get rid of Joseph permanently. They seemed to be driven by a need for affiliation (n Aff) so that they could get close to their father and find favour in Jacob's eyes again.

Such a traumatic event robbed Joseph of approximately twenty-three years of family life. He was ripped from his father, and Benjamin, his full brother. This new fate, along with the fact that his mother had died a few years earlier, rendered him an apparent hopeless orphan. The psychological abuse which occurred in his youthful age was enough to instigate Joseph to be angry, bitter and hostile. This was enough to awaken negative emotions in one's heart. Furthermore, he was alone in a foreign country. The Joseph we encountered earlier continued to be in the spot light even in his new 'homeland'. Notably, his life was more tumultuous than when he was with his brothers.

While he worked for his master, Joseph became a hunted and greatly sought-after potential playboy for his master's wife. Having refused to play her games, his life took another twist and he was banished away to a dungeon as a prisoner. However, I wonder what processes would we have to go through in order to develop the emotional capacity to forgive and reconcile with the person who hurt us? At the outset, this chapter is grounded on the first section of following principle: *To forgive, a person needs to experience some degree of healing; and to experience healing, an individual needs to forgive herself and others.* In focusing on the view that in order to forgive, you must experience some degree of healing on emotional, psychological and spiritual levels, I propose that an individual's emotional and spiritual healing proceeds through three processes: (1) the initial process of preparing the path; (2) the intermediate process of self-disclosure, and (3) consolidating the healing.

INITIAL PROCESS: PREPARING THE PATH

It had seemed almost certain that Joseph would be lost in prison for eternity. But divine providence prepared the path for his deliverance and ultimately, for his emotional healing. The writer of this biblical saga reminds us of his prison life in Egypt when he continued to be favoured by various leaders. By the time Pharaoh, the Egyptian King, had a sleepless night from a troubling dream, divine providence once again emerged and allowed Joseph to be in the spot light by being a specialist in interpreting dreams. The King, on hearing about Joseph's special spiritually-endowed gift, demanded that he be brought out of the dungeon. It was the miraculous means by which he was delivered from the dark, desolate dungeon.

Moreover, the initial encounter between Joseph and his brothers and their interaction in Egypt also contributed to paving the path for the emotional healing to occur. Scripture recounts that chilling encounter: "Now Joseph was the governor of the land, the person who sold grain to all its people. So when Joseph's brothers arrived, they bowed down to him with their faces to the ground. As soon as Joseph saw his brothers, he recognized them, but he pretended to be a stranger and spoke harshly to them. 'Where do you come from?' he asked. 'From the land of Canaan,' they replied, 'to buy food.' Although Joseph recognized his brothers, they did not recognize him. Then he remembered his dreams about them and said to them, 'You are spies! You have come to see where our land is unprotected.' 'No, my lord,' they answered. 'Your servants have come to buy food. We are all the sons of one man. Your servants are honest men, not spies.' 'No!' he said to them. You have come to see where our land is unprotected.' But they replied, 'Your servants were twelve brothers, the sons of one man, who lives in the land of Canaan. The youngest is now with our father, and one is no more' (Gen 42: 6-13, NIV). Unknowingly and unwittingly, the brothers played into the hands of the circumspect Joseph. What was Joseph's degree of emotional wounded-ness? Was he bruised, wounded, broken or damaged? It is certain that Joseph had been travelling *on the road to forgiveness.*

BOX 9.1: THINKING ANALYTICALLY

Ms P, age eighty, who has been married and divorced twice, has been having trouble with her six adult children. Of these six, only one of them visits her, even though she hears from four others. Her last daughter has not seen her mother for years, neither has she been calling her. However, a few months before her eightieth birthday, mum took sick and was hospitalised for a few days. Every day the medical team promised to send her home, but her illness got worst. At this news, she summoned all of her children to the hospital. Although the youngest daughter came to the hospital ward, she refused to approach her at her bedside. In the far distance, her mother called out for her to come nearer, but she refused. The sick mother's arm was outstretched to welcome her daughter. Tears trickled down the faces of mum and her baby daughter. Years of anger, animosity, hatred and hostility surged in their hearts. Mum confided that these were tears of hurt and relief.

Pause with me at this time. On examining this case, at least three major issues emerged: loss, poor parent-child interpersonal relationships and the impact of illness. Ms P, who has been divorced twice, has experienced a loss in her marriages. Perhaps forgiveness has never been extended, a situation which could have left her broken. Furthermore, with most of her children being estranged from her, this has brought about another loss. This transpired into an apparent irreparable damage of the parent-child relationship, to the extent that there was no interaction between her and most of the children.

Individuals who experience any kind of loss, invariably tends to grieve. These types of losses elicit a number of questions: What was the divorce experience like for her? Was it amicable? Divisive? Hostile? Stormy? Was Ms P still grieving? Was she ever compensated or given alimony after the divorces? How did the children respond to the divorces? Did they lack a father-figure? Did they blame their mother for the termination of the marriages? Is it worth the effort to continue holding the mother by 'her throat' for the break-up of the home? If the poor relationships are to be used as a guide, it seems that there are visible open wounds which need healing. Furthermore, some of the children seem to be emotionally stuck, hence a possible reason for the estrangement. In order for emotional progress to be made, forgiveness must be extended and received, thereby helping with the healing process.

The second issue of poor parent-child interpersonal relationship has evolved into a flood of negative emotions being distributed. The moods and feelings seemed to be rooted in a source that has not been uncovered or exposed. Such an experience perhaps has had a negative effect on Ms P over the years. With most of the children not making contact with their mother, and with the display of these negative emotions in their adult life, this suggests that this family could be psychologically dysfunctional. It would be advantageous to provide an opportunity for the children to detoxify themselves, thereby preparing the path to restore the relationship with their mother.

Ms P's illness and prolonged hospitalization seemed to have awakened the thought of death in her mind, thus leading to her calling for all her children to visit her. The uncertainty of her recuperation could also have been an opportunity for her to reach out to her children and gain some measure of contact. Additionally, it would be spiritually uplifting for mum to invite a religious pastoral care-giver to assist with the healing process. It seems very likely that she was experiencing a sense of guilt and did not want to die with it on her mind. Having analysed this case, we can conclude that Ms P's hospitalization, and sickness played a significant role, in that, they prepared the path for healing to begin between her and the children. Additionally, the crying is an essential aspect of one's healing process, seeing that it allows the individual to offload the emotional hurt in another form. Although the act of crying is not a verbal response, its audible nature is effective in contributing to a degree of healing.

In returning to the story of Joseph and his brothers, the heated and harsh verbal exchange allowed the ten brothers to confess their sinful deeds openly and admit that they were guilty of mis-treating Joseph in the past. It is at this point that the motif of 'Joseph's weeping' emerges with important significance for the fourth stage of the *on the road to forgiveness*. During this period of the journey, Joseph wept twice, perhaps signifying the depth of his sorrow in seeing his siblings fall into his hands.[68] The tense encounter exposed everyone, particularly Joseph, who was in tears. Were these tears of anger, humility, jubilation or sadness? On further reflection, this first round of weeping could be tears of empathy in relation to his dream that the entire family would bow down to him. In fact, Joseph could have been weeping because he saw the divinely orchestrated dream being fulfilled and recognised that his siblings may have been too blind to perceive the Omnipotent Hand in his life.

Meanwhile, the brothers were in distress on account of the concealed guilt rising to the surface. Nevertheless, Bill T. Arnold observes that the scene depicting the encounter between Joseph and his brothers was unbearable, thus forcing Joseph to become emotional and by extension, to weep. Arnold, however, contends that Joseph was uncertain as to how much he could trust his brothers and therefore, held back the vital intelligence about his identity.[69] Time is necessary for him to observe any semblance of transformation in his once-upon-a-time cold-hearted and devious siblings. Interestingly, Westermann suggests that their act of confessing the evil deed against Joseph brought about freedom and by extension, created new situations. He noted that the act identified one understanding of confession based on one's experience. Westermann, on reflected further observed that the brothers were inspired by a greater power.[70] This interaction between Joseph and his brothers brought about an awakening which stirred their hearts.

However, it would appear that Joseph, having undergone a gruelling and horrifying ordeal, had been transformed because of the divine favour and providence in his life while living in Potiphar's house.[71] At this juncture in his life, he seemed to have experienced some degree of emotional, psychological and spiritual healing. It was this regenerated state that would have been responsible for him being able to move on with his life. Thus, he was prepared for the moment which required him to extend horizontal forgiveness. He seemed to be eager to clear the path and initiate the healing of the breach in the relationship between himself and his brothers. Additionally, Joseph seemed to have been overwhelmed by the turn of events in his siblings' lives who appeared unaware of the fulfilment of the divinely pronounced dream about his life. His tearful reaction seems to be beyond the superficial. Clare Amos concludes that Joseph's moments of weeping brought about a gradual built-up opportunity for reconciliation with his siblings.[72] More and more Joseph continuous display of emotions "points more clearly than could any words to that which is the main point - the wholeness of a society *[or an individual]* and what that means for those who belong to it."[73] His experience *on the road to forgiveness* helped to prepare the path. Have you begun the journey towards forgiveness? Have you prepared the path towards experiencing a time of healing? Are there still issues blocking the path of your journey? How eager are you to experience healing on all levels? A major factor in being healed emotionally is to be willing to adopt safe vulnerability and engage in self-disclosure.

INTERMEDIATE PROCESS: SELF-DISCLOSURE

The final three sentences of Genesis 43 summarise the state of play between Joseph and his brothers. Similar to a united and functional family/ household, all of Joseph's brothers, his Egyptian officials, along with Joseph, sat around the large dining table at meal time. It resembled an emotionally whole group who are co-operative and peaceful, thus, cultivating an air of purpose about them. It displayed a sense of orderliness among the brothers who were seated in order of age, all of who elatedly were enjoying a fellowship meal. We cannot read this without concluding that this is the type of scene Joseph had missed out on for more than two decades. The family time of old was an opportunity to catch up with the progress of the farm. It was a time to share with their parents some of their adventurous manoeuvres in the fields while looking after the flock. Family time is an occasion to be merry and to laugh. It is a time to address the burning issues that have been festering for a long time. However, on a more profound level, the two earlier occasions when Joseph wept lamentably and secretly, were times which also prepared the path for emotional and spiritual healing. The scene of a sumptuous meal and vivacious laughter at the table suggested that some degree of healing had occurred.

Having moved on emotionally and being saddled with the desire and responsibility of revealing himself, Joseph, the biblical character, disclosed his true identity to his brothers. Immediately, the true character of a previously emotionally-wounded individual, who has experienced some degree of healing, flashed before the brothers' eyes. Having reminded them of their mis-treatment towards him, Joseph humbly declared that he was their 'lost' brother. Moreover, he re-assured them that no harm would come their way and compassionately encouraged them not to think about any repercussions. Individuals similar to Joseph who experience healing, would have undergone a transformation. It is essential that we arrive at this stage in our journey through which we can extend horizontal forgiveness. Such individuals reach a stage on this journey when they reach a crossroad. They must decide whether they will remain bitter, hostile and revengeful or display a divinely-instigated transformation and extend forgiveness.

Of the six times this biblical character was in tears, this is the second round of weeping.[74] His crying became more intense perhaps because of the long delay in keeping his true identity from his suffering brothers. It could be that he perceived that they were emotionally distraught and with the opportunity for revenge being in his hands, he was torn between two minds. Nevertheless, on greeting his only full brother, whom he had not seen for more than two decades, they seemed to experienced emotional closure by engaging in minimal effective response (MER).

Emotional closure occurs when a victim has had an opportunity to be heard and to share his emotional pain and the impact of the issue on him. Evidence of this experience in this biblical saga is seen when Joseph 'mis-treated' his brothers by placing them in prison, speaking to them harshly at first and accusing them of being spes.

> **Minimal effective response mechanisms (MERs) are the least psychological actions or behaviours which a hurting individual exhibits in an attempt to find emotional closure.**

Additionally, further evidence of emotional closure is seen in his weeping and in his explanation of the turn of events in his life. Although Joseph resurrected his brothers' previous mistreatment towards him, he attributed it to divine providence and identified it as the divine purpose for his entire family's survival.[75] Furthermore, the actions Joseph took may seem to have been extensive, extreme and harsh, but these were the actions Joseph used as his MERs which were necessary to give him the emotional closure. More importantly, they were the most beneficial actions, which allowed him an opportunity for emotional resolution in his life. These were the least morally appropriate actions he could have undertaken in order to feel vindicated, to feel a sense of justice and to be liberated from the emotional 'prison' in which he was living for a long time.

The desire to experience emotional and psychological closure is an inborn desire to resolve the uncertainty and ambiguity which have emerged after a conflict or negative experience. Individuals, who lack the opportunity to experience closure, may struggle frequently by contemplating on how an experience could have played out differently in order to bring about a different outcome. However, on experiencing closure, emotionally-affected individuals are no longer haunted by those troubling feelings. This opportunity, therefore, contributes to the individuals' huge emotional burdens being relieved.

BOX 9.2: THINKING ANALYTICALLY

Ms P's last daughter blamed her mother for the incest between her and her step-father. This traumatic event had left deep emotional scars, prolonged unhealed pain and deep confusion in the daughter's life. Mum tried to apologise, but it brought more tears. On seeing her estranged daughter, Ms P, tried to assure her that all was going to be well. She alerted her daughter that the past was in the past and she was willing to put it behind her and move on. In her state of physical weakness, mum explained that during the girl's horrendous ordeal, she was experiencing physical abuse. The other children, horrified and shocked at the revelation of this news, broke down again in tears.

Take a moment to engage in some analytical thinking. This other aspect of Ms. P's case is an example of a dysfunctional and toxic family producing a toxic child in the youngest daughter. It is as a result of the barrage of negative emotions which emerged from mum and her 'baby' daughter, among other issues. However, the major issues emerging are: forms of abuse, unaddressed emotional issues and the impact of family secrets. Since some members of this family have suffered from both physical and sexual abuse, clearly there is a need for counselling, along with the input of a religious pastoral care-giver who is equipped to apply various spiritual resources such as intercessory prayer and the application of the Holy Scriptures. Since the youngest daughter's wounds are still open, the blaming attitude will not cease. It would be useful to help the daughter de-clutter and flush her emotional self of the traumatic event by undergoing therapy. Help can also be gained by engaging in spiritual disciplines such as prayer and fasting along with other therapeutic treatments.

Abuse in any form is a traumatic experience which results in the victim entering the fight, flight or freezing mode. In this case, the last daughter seemed to have entered the freezing mode in that she is covered with confusion, pain and scars, all of which seem to contribute to her inability to forgive or interact with her mother, and therefore, she seems to be emotionally stuck. This psychological state indicates that individuals who are affected by the emotionally-stuck syndrome have a mental understanding of their goals and desires, but emotionally they do not feel confident or equipped to accomplish their personal achievements. This implies that such persons' internal lives are on hold, and their coping and problem-solving skills are affected negatively, even though such individuals may seem to be active externally.

Although Ms P tried to appease the situation, this aspect of the case has brought out various unaddressed emotional issues. One is forced to ask a number of pertinent questions: Was there any support available which the youngest daughter could have accessed? Did she understand the critical nature of her traumatic experience? How was she able to live with these wounds for such a long time? Did the other siblings know about their sister's abuse? How did mum cope with her own traumatic situation? What coping mechanisms did she use? When we consider various types of coping strategies, the last daughter used a maladaptive approach by staying away from her mother for almost a lifetime. While this could have been helpful in avoiding the 'environment' which caused her emotional pain, it did not bring healing because she did not face the situation, nor surrendered it. Her attitude towards her mother indicated that she was still living in the past and therefore, needed help in escaping this destructive mode of existence.

The third issue relates to Ms P's experience of physical abuse which has been kept hidden from her children for decades. With the children breaking down in tears, it implies that this situation was never mentioned nor discussed, hence classifying it as a family secret. It appears that Ms P felt that by withholding this information from her children, she was protecting them. In fact, it created a chasm and division among them. Family secrets produce destructive effects, one of which is estrangement, as is evident in this case. Furthermore, she has lived with this secret for many decades, which no doubt could have impacted negatively on her interaction with the children.

Although there was a measure of self-disclosure among the members of this family, a counsellor or therapist would be beneficial in assisting them with facing these situations and sharing them openly. Additionally, counselling sessions could help them in surrendering the issues through processes such as writing therapy or gestalt therapy. Individuals who seek to extend forgiveness and experience healing are at an advantage when they go through this intermediate process of engaging in self-disclosure. Although self-disclosure may be painful, it ultimately aids in the healing process, thereby, enabling individuals to take the journey *on the road to forgiveness.*

I now revert to the tearful episode between Joseph and his brothers. Bill T. Arnold suggests that Joseph's boisterous and audible tears had emerged because of the news which he had shared about his identity and also because of the brotherly affection he had developed for his siblings.[76] Seeing that the brothers talked with him, it signalled the end of estrangement and emotional distance. The significance of the weeping motif emerges in this intermediary process, to the extent that weeping is an effective means by which individuals can proceed through stages of reconciliation and healing.[77] In revealing himself to his brothers and assuring them that all was well, Joseph extended forgiveness to them, an act which aided the healing process, and by extension, contributed to a reconciliatory reunion which was based on the display of interpersonal forgiveness.[78] Such actions suggest that he displayed 'safe vulnerability', a quality which required him to expose himself emotionally, but yet he had the capacity to manage the after-effects of the disclosure. Such character traits are necessary for experiencing some degree of healing so that we can extend forgiveness and bring about reconciliation with others where possible.

FINAL PROCESS: CONSOLIDATING THE HEALING

The penultimate episode in the book of Genesis reminds us that our emotional wellbeing fluctuates because of the numerous encounters we experience with other hurting people. Joseph's brothers had experienced a loss on two occasions: the enslavement of Joseph for more than a decade and the death of their father. However, during the period of mourning their father's death, there were still carrying partially open wounds which needed healing. Experiences such as these, suggest that individuals who embark on becoming emotionally healed must seek to consolidate the process. This can be achieved by displaying a compassionate heart and reinforcing the act of forgiveness.

Three critical issues emerge from this episode. First, the brothers attempted to engage in deceptive behaviour again, by using their dead father's name as leverage to obtain forgiveness. By creating a false message, they directly asked to be forgiven of the evil deed which was still lingering over their 'heads'. Desperation leads individuals to engage in unorthodox behaviours at any cost. However, the biblical writer, on reiterating the brothers' evil deed towards Joseph, highlights the severity of the heinous crime the boys had committed. Perhaps the intensity of the sin contributed to it being highlighted again, hence a possible factor for their constant obsession with how Joseph would treat them. Although the brothers' intentions were to bring an end to their life-long destructive attitude, their prevailing view of Joseph seemed to have aggravated the slowly healing situation, thus making it worst.

Second, the brothers were haunted by an imaginary hatred in Joseph's heart. It appeared as though they were obsessed with experiencing an emotional 'backlash' because of their historic mis-treatment towards Joseph. It could be that the brothers were projecting their prolonged deep-seated hatred onto Joseph as a defence mechanism. Nevertheless, the various interactions from previous episodes indicated that Joseph had forgiven his brothers and was free of negative feelings towards them. Ellen G. White observed that "after the burial of Jacob, fear again filled the hearts of Joseph's brothers. Notwithstanding his kindness toward them, their conscious guilt was staring them in the face and haunting them. It made them distrustful and suspicious. It might be that he had delayed his revenge, out of regard to their father, and that he would now visit upon them the long-deferred punishment for their crime. … This message affected Joseph to tears, and, encouraged by this, his brothers came and fell down before him, with the words, Joseph's love for his brothers was deep and unselfish, and he was pained at the thought that they could regard him as cherishing a spirit of revenge toward them."[79] The final occasion when Joseph wept bitterly indicates that he was awakened once more by divine providence in his life, even though the brothers' evil deeds stared him in his face which was still full of love for them.[80] Joseph's profound love for his siblings inspired him to help them rise from the 'pit of fear' which seems to be haunting them. In dealing with his erring brothers compassionately, Joseph was able to consolidate the healing process, thereby assisting everyone in moving forward emotionally, psychologically, socially and spiritually.

Third, the brothers were paralysed by a fearful spirit. They seemed to have been tortured and troubled perhaps because there was no longer anyone to intercede on their behalf and protect them from Joseph's possible desire for revenge. But, the innocent brother compassionately counselled them repeatedly not to become terrified. What could have instigated this fear in their hearts? Had they repented honestly of their former deed? Was there unconditional love in their hearts for their brother? Having been reunited with Joseph for approximately eighty years, what issues could have prevented the brothers from developing a loving relationship with Joseph?[81] In spite of the brothers' attitude, Joseph reinforced the act of forgiveness by highlighting the impact of divine providence in his life. He attributed his painful ordeal to the fulfilment of the divine will for the preservation of his entire family of origin. Thus, he re-assured his siblings by displaying a forgiving attitude which was manifested in his behaviour and final treatment towards them.

In taking a biblical perspective of the brothers' fearful attitude, we are reminded that "as we live in God, our *love* grows more perfect. So we will not be afraid on the Day of Judgment, but we can face him with confidence because we live like Jesus here in this world. Such *love* has no fear, because perfect *love* expels all fear. If we are afraid, it is for fear of punishment, and this shows that we have not fully experienced his perfect *love*."[82] The tension between love and fear suggests that individuals who fear a person are unable to trust that feared individual since he/she may not have developed a loving relationship with the other person. Nevertheless, in order for emotional and spiritual healing to occur, we must address the issues which contribute to the presence of fear, hatred and other destructive emotions in our lives. It is a vital undertaking which is necessary to consolidate our healing. Having reached this stage of our journey *on the road to forgiveness*, it is essential that we take further steps to demonstrate our willingness to move further ahead in every aspect of our life.

SUMMARY

The discussion in this chapter has been based on the first section of the following principle: *to forgive, a person needs to experience some degree of healing, and to experience healing, an individual needs to forgive herself and others.* Of the three processes contributing to experiencing emotional and spiritual healing, the first process of preparing the path consists of moments of weeping. Biblical, experiential and psychological evidence indicate that tears are significant to one's healing process, in that they provide an outlet by which individuals can express their inner emotions. Self-disclosure is the main focus of the intermediate process and involves experiencing emotional closure through minimal effective responses. Emotional closure for emotionally-distressed individuals is essential, in that it aids in clarifying any uncertainties about the negative experience and also provides a sense of finality to the issue(s). In order for one's emotional and spiritual healing to be sealed, it must be consolidated. This process can occur by displaying compassion and by re-assuring the perpetrator that she has been forgiven. This stage in the journey helps individuals to develop their emotional capacity so that they can progress emotionally and spiritually.

10

DEVELOPING YOUR EMOTIONAL CAPACITY TO MOVE ON

The twenty-first verse of the last chapter of Genesis reveals that Joseph, the protagonist, has experienced a transformed heart, out of which he has displayed real human compassion. The speech to and the interaction with his brothers indicate a sense of emotional and psychological closure for him: "Now therefore, do not be afraid. I will provide for *and* support you and your little ones. And he comforted them [imparting cheer, hope, strength] and spoke to their hearts [kindly]."[83] Individuals who display a forgiving attitude similar to that of Joseph would have experienced some degree of emotional and spiritual healing, which enables them to move on emotionally.

This significant verse demonstrates that emotional progress had been made. The same Joseph in the beginning of the saga kind-heartedly provides food for his scheming siblings. It is the same Joseph who vowed to provide for his siblings, now that he is at the end of his life. The jovial, peaceful Joseph is more composed, matured and spiritual at the end of the story. He has taken the spotlight again, while his brothers faded away into the background. Nevertheless, everyone has moved on emotionally and spiritually. The story's plot has shifted from the exhibition of angry attitudes and a display of negative emotions to a time of hope. Having addressed the issues surrounding his brothers and himself, in the end, Joseph channelled his energies into looking after his immediate family of origin.

But this dramatic 'rags to riches' saga demonstrates that emotional difficulties distract individuals from experiencing personal development and holistic progress in their lives. Emotional difficulties absorb our emotional energy, slow us down and create barriers. They rob individuals of essential time. Emotional difficulties are like animal or plant parasites, which feed on another organism and cause great damage to the host. But unless the parasite is dealt with, it can destroy the host organism.

In the penultimate scene of this story, we recognise that emotional and spiritual progress has been made in relation to Joseph's journey. Nevertheless, in order to continue travelling on the road to forgiveness, it is important that we develop our emotional capacity. One way by which this can be achieved is by focusing on the ultimate goal and move forward emotionally and spiritually. This points us to the final stage of this journey which is based on the following principle: *emotional and spiritual healing create a desire to move on.*

Individuals, who reach this stage on the road to forgiveness as seen in Fig. 10.1, tend to experience profound emotional and spiritual progress.

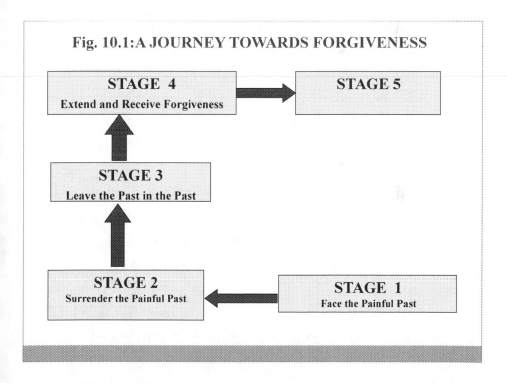

Fig. 10.1:A JOURNEY TOWARDS FORGIVENESS

Their progress and healing can be reinforced by engaging in the following steps: a) give assurance of optimal forgiveness, (b) strive towards your divinely-imparted potential and (c) be aware of the impact of contrasting spirituality.

STEP 1: GIVE ASSURANCE OF OPTIMAL FORGIVENESS

Individuals who have a profound desire to progress emotionally need to assure the other person that she has been forgiven completely and wholeheartedly. This involves totally surrendering the desire for revenge and seeking to experience a measure of healing. It is essential for individuals, who want to move on emotionally, to ensure that they are emotionally free, to the point that they develop positive emotions, while seeking the transformation of negative ones. Since the heart is the seat of our emotions and passions, individuals can benefit from monitoring their inner feelings about the painful issues they have experienced. At times we attempt to convince ourselves that we have addressed the issue and that we have moved on with our lives, but our attitudes and behaviours tend to indicate otherwise.

To explain the need for complete forgiveness, I share the following illustration. About six years after Ms Dr and Mrs. K became close friends, Ms Dr told a lie on her close and trusted friend, Mrs. K. In trying to resolve the issue, Ms Dr refused to apologise on the basis that she simply was sharing a situation that seemed to have occurred. Mrs. K felt disappointed, hurt and rejected. Mrs. K desperately attempted to alert Ms Dr of how her behaviour had affected her. However, Ms Dr explained that she did not intend to hurt her friend. Nevertheless, she emphatically refused to back down or to change her story. Well, by taking this attitude, Ms Dr had bought a proverbial 'bottle of poison' called "un-forgiveness" and gave it to Mrs. K to drink, without anticipating the consequences. In a cold, harsh and inconsiderate demeanour, Ms Dr actually drank the 'bottle of poison' herself and began to die slowly. Any attitude, we display short of total forgiveness, is detrimental to us, in that, it destroys us to the point of bringing about emotional and even physical death.

Scripture aptly reminds us that "the *heart* is deceitful above all things, And desperately wicked; who can know it? I, the LORD, search the *heart*, I test the mind, even to give every man according to his ways, according to the fruit of his doings."[84] Prior to the appearance of the above-mentioned verse in Jeremiah 17, the writer of this biblical book uses the Hebrew term [lebab] for 'heart' more than a dozen times in the previous chapters. The context in which this term has been used relates to un-Christlike affections, attitudes and thoughts which have led to the presence of undesirable behaviours in people's hearts. The heart motif in the book of Jeremiah portrays a spiritually distressing state, in which people are incapable of leading a spiritually matured life. In fact, within this spiritual context in the book of Jeremiah, individuals are instructed to desist from following the evil dictates of their own heart such as encouraging bitterness and being rebellious towards people in authority.

The *New Living Translation* version of this text portrays the human condition in this way: "The human heart is the most deceitful of all things, and desperately wicked. Who really knows how bad it is? But I, the LORD, search all hearts and examine secret motives. I give all people their due rewards, according to what their actions deserve." On examining the language used in this version, we cannot help but recognise the evil tendencies of the heart, the centre of an individual's thoughts. Actually, words such as 'bad', 'deceitful', and 'wicked' convey this perspective and demonstrate the morally corrupt nature of the heart. Other linguistic features which describe the nature of the heart denote that it is also exceedingly weak, desperately sick or frail. These different understandings of the nature of the heart suggest that it is impossible to rely on the faithfulness of the 'heart'. In essence, we recognise that in order to move forward on an emotional and spiritual level, it is essential that we seek to extend forgiveness fully to those who have wronged us. On reflection, have you forgiven your perpetrator sincerely? What do you think about when you see your opponent? Do you have the emotional capacity to forgive your opponent?

Let's examine the final aspect of Ms P's case which reveals the impact of un-forgiveness on relationships. The sharp contention, the cold, distant and non-existing relationship between Ms P and her youngest daughter reveals three issues: broken trust, psychological dysfunctionality and emotional wounded-ness. First, the last daughter expected her mother to be there for her, but this did not happen, thus leading to a breakdown in trust. It would appear that the last daughter felt that Ms P was encouraging the abuse, by not speaking out or seeking appropriate help. The lack of trust on the youngest daughter's part and the distant relationship with her mother suggest that there was a sense of

---

BOX 10.1: THINKING ANALYTICALLY

Ms P's older daughter recognised that the strained relationship between her mother and her baby sister had existed for too long. She intervened and encouraged both of them to admit that there were problems. Mum, in tears, apologised for failing her last daughter during her formative years when she was growing up. She also shared her inability to address the traumatic situation and the presence of emotional weakness, all of which prevented her from talking about or preventing the various forms of abuse. By now, the daughter having approached the bed-side, fell on her mother's neck and cried bitterly. The other sisters and brothers were wide-eyed and stood in awe. Having asked to be forgiven, the youngest daughter shared that she felt betrayed for many years, but she was now at the point of being willing to move forward. This brought reconciliation between the two of them. All the children hugged each other, as they wept on each other's shoulders. Soon after, mum was relieved. A few days later, Ms P was released from hospital and has been well ever since that time.

---

disgust, a secondary emotion, which emerges from being angry about an issue or with someone. It appears that this anger, a primary emotion, was built up over the years to the point that she developed hatred and revulsion for her mother, hence another possible reason she never visited her.

The second issue relates to psychological dysfunctionality in this family. In particular, the youngest daughter's need for love and belonging was unmet for a prolonged period of time. This unfulfilled need has led to the emotional distress present in these two family members. The display of anger, bitter feelings and hatred over a long period of time is evidence of the dysfunctionality which exists. Consequently, the daughter's safety needs were compromised due to incest and therefore, not considered. This could have been the reason for her love and belonging needs being unfulfilled, in that, the lower level needs were unmet. Additionally, it could be that the youngest daughter refused to approach her mother's bedside at the hospital because she was stuck at the safety needs and felt she still could not trust her mother who had betrayed and refused to protect her during her childhood and teenage years. The emotional distress could also have occurred due to an unstable home environment which consisted of abusive and untrusted parents.

Emotional wounded-ness is another issue which has emerged in this case. Based on the data in the case, the youngest daughter's sense of security has been shattered deeply and she has been confused due to her parents' irresponsible behaviour. Furthermore, she withdrew from and totally avoided any contact with her mother, whose presence would have reminded her of the traumatic abusive situation. It appears that having seen her mother on the hospital ward, this may have brought back terrifying memories and flashbacks about the emotionally-difficult situation from the past. These features are symptomatic of a person who is emotionally damaged, the most profound level of emotional wounded-ness, thus suggesting that the youngest daughter has been experiencing negative emotional health.

In focusing on the task of building up our emotional capacity, it is important that we fully address, with sincerity from the heart, any issues relating to un-forgiveness. Such an attitude equips us with the capacity to strive towards our divine potential. What could be hindering you from progressing further at the emotional and spiritual levels? Having reached this stage of the journey towards forgiveness, what issues are you still struggling with at this point? Do you have the resources to help you reach the place where you are able to engage in horizontal forgiveness?

STEP 2: STRIVE TOWARDS YOUR DIVINELY-IMPARTED POTENTIAL

Although it was important for Joseph to reach forward and develop his divinely-imparted potential, he existed in an atmosphere of suspicion and mistrust. These negative affective elements have the potential to destroy one's ability to progress emotionally. However, individuals, on experiencing some degree of healing, are encouraged to move forward emotionally. To reach this place in our life, requires that we focus on achieving the ultimate major goal. This can be acquired in three processes: a) display kindness to one's opponent; (b) demonstrate compassion and (c) speak kindly from the heart. First, individuals who have experienced some degree of emotional healing can strive towards their divinely-imparted potential by displaying kindness to their opponent. When we think of kindness, it denotes being considerate or helpful to others. It is a quality which conveys generous attitude, humane, sympathetic, and warm-hearted. Furthermore, individuals display kindness when they have experienced a deep sense of satisfaction in their life.

Reverting to Joseph's emotional ordeal, we notice evidence of kindness demonstrated to his brothers. Scripture recounts the conversation between Joseph and his brothers: "I will provide for *and* support you and your little ones" (Gen 50:21b, AMP). The twenty-first verse of Genesis 50 reveals Joseph acting from a renewed heart. It is a consolidation of the same sentiments he had expressed earlier in relation to providing for his siblings, thus demonstrating his willingness to care for and be kind to them.[85] Having undergone such a renewal, he displayed an unselfish concern for his emotionally-shattered siblings. Moreover, his willingness to cater to their physical needs highlights that he possessed a benevolent and charitable heart.

When we experience emotional and spiritual freedom, we gain the capacity to think of others and assist in meeting their needs. On further examining the details in this episode, we become aware that Joseph focused on his brothers' physiological needs by assuring them that food will be provided for them. By providing for his brothers, Joseph was determined to nourish, support and sustain them with food. With Joseph focusing on this basic need, it suggests that his brothers were at the bottom of the hierarchy of psychological needs and therefore, had a deficiency which was obstructing them from rising emotionally.

Individuals who have experienced emotional, psychological or spiritual healing are capable of sharing with wounded people, thus gaining the experience to become wounded healers. In fact, healed people present a healing atmosphere around themselves. Attitudes are renewed. Behaviours are reshaped. Habits are revised. Thoughts are transformed. Such inner renewal contributes to the development of one's emotional capacity to move on. A transformation is essential for ensuring that emotional and spiritual progress is achieved. In so doing, this helps us to reach the final stage on the road towards forgiveness

Second, comforting those who are emotionally-distressed is an effective process in this last stage on the road to forgiveness. When we comfort others, we display compassion towards them because of a devastating experience which they may have undergone. It involves providing physical case and ensuring that they are free from pain or constraint. Moreover, it relates to easing or alleviating a person's grief or distress. Such an example prevails in Genesis 50, where the biblical writer alerts us of Joseph's attitude to his brothers.[86] Here, his compassion for his brothers was understandable and even predictable. One factor to be considered is that they were mourning the death of their father which brought about extensive grief and a profound loss. Furthermore, the death created a chasm since there was no one to be mediator between them and Joseph. This realisation could have compounded their sorrow, thus, another reason for considering the display of compassion to be understandable.

Another factor accounting for the predictability of Joseph's compassion towards his brothers is that they were in a foreign country and indirectly controlled by Pharaoh, King of Egypt. From all accounts, they did not set out to stay in this foreign country so long, let alone experience their father dying so quickly. Scripture is silent on their views about being in Egypt for that length of time. Perhaps they were not in a positive emotional state to comment on their purpose in Egypt. Numerous troubling questions may have been going through their minds: How soon will the famine come to end? What is Joseph's ultimate reason for showing kindness? How probable is it to stay permanently in Egypt? Should we pack up and return to Canaan? Such realities could have been brought to the surface knowing that these issues could have impacted the brothers' lives.

When we reflect on how Joseph comforted his brothers by displaying affectionate compassion towards them, we are pointed to the inspiring instructions in the biblical book of Romans which catalogues the attitude a Christian believer should display towards others.[87] In Chapter12, the author identifies a number of Christian virtues such as kindness, longsuffering and love which should be exhibited in one's life. Actually, these are a sample of the list of the fruit of the Holy Spirit as identified in Galatians 5, thus suggesting that individuals, who compassionately comfort others, are inspired divinely to act in this way.[88] Additionally, Christian believers are instructed to engage in service by meeting the needs of others. Having provided the theological foundation for comforting others, the biblical writer proceeds to outline practical ways by which individuals can be comforted.[89] In particular, celebrating with others, living peacefully among individuals and refraining from taking revenge are ways by which individuals, who have experienced emotional healing, can be compassionate to those who have hurt them.

Pause with me at this time and consider the theme prevailing in the episodes surrounding Joseph and his brothers in the book of Genesis. The theme of safety runs seamlessly throughout the various sub-episodes ranging from personal safety from danger to security from retribution. During the encounter between Joseph and his brothers in Chapter 37, some of the siblings were concerned about his personal safety seeing that their hatred for him had instigated them to kill him (Genesis 37:18-24). And although they did not kill him, yet they banished him into non-existence from his father's home by selling him to a group of merchants, who eventually sold him to an Egyptian palace official. Everyone craves for safety. We hunger for safety from gun crimes, harassment on the job, professional pretentious beggars, sexual predators, thieves or violent gangs. Being safe in our environment, be it on the job, in a business office or at home, allows us to be focused on other important issues, thereby, aiding us in being effective in our task. Based on this view, the brothers may have perceived Joseph as a threat, hence the reason for getting rid of him.

By the time we reach the episode with Potiphar's wife, who attempted unsuccessfully to ensnare Joseph, we are in no doubt that safety is a very prominently theme. With Joseph being a slave to Potiphar, an officer of King Pharaoh and also being the captain of the guard, the calculated chances of Potiphar's wife succeeding were high. In fact, since "she kept putting pressure on Joseph day after day, ... [and] he refused to sleep with her, and he kept out of her way as much as possible" (Gen 39:10, NLT), he was not safe around her. Intimate boundaries were being attacked, ignored and even forcibly violated, to the point that he had to escape for his life. Such passion-driven pursuits indicate that we need to be protected from individuals who possess untransformed minds, since they seem to be propelled to fulfil their needs at any cost.

With the saga progressing speedily, Joseph was incarcerated in a royal prison for political prisoners. Here in this situation, he desperately pleaded with his prison companions, namely the chief butler and the chief baker. Scripture reveals this yearning interaction, with the *Amplified* version depicting Joseph's profound craving for release: "But think of me when it shall be well with you and show kindness, I beg of you, to me, and mention me to Pharaoh and get me out of this house. For truly I was carried away from the land of the Hebrews by unlawful force, and here too I have done nothing for which they should put me into the dungeon" (Gen 40:14-15). The details indicate that he was left in the dungeon, and the butler, having moved on, forgot about Joseph's request (Gen 40:23). One cannot help but believe that Joseph was concerned about his physical safety, knowing that political prisoners usually were executed immediately. And although this two-time unlawfully imprisoned slave tried to pull the 'innocence' card with the butler, it was too obscure to be seen.

The sub-episodes from Genesis 42 until the end of the book continue to portray the theme of safety. However, the narrator has shifted to the safety of the brothers. They were incarcerated (Gen 42:17), haunted by guilt (Gen 42:21-22; 44:16) and paralysed by fear (Gen 50:19, 21). Such situations echo the need for safety on the emotional, physical and psychological levels, and therefore, require that this need be fulfilled. With this being the case, the brothers were willing to meet this need at any cost, to the point that they co-operated with all of Joseph's demands, and even tried to be deceptive again in the end.

Moreover, on deeper reflection, we observe that Joseph benefitted from divine providence which brought predominantly physical protection. This form of safety, which portrays extensive divine input, prevails throughout this entire biblical saga. In fact, it is this ingredient that aids Joseph in developing his emotional and spiritual capacity to move forward *on the road to forgiveness.* Ultimately, individuals who seek to absorb the divine teachings on forgiveness into their lives could experience the emotional, psychological and spiritual victories they long for during their journey.

Third, speaking kindly to your opponents is another effective process necessary for striving towards our divinely-imparted potential. In speaking kindly we assure our enemies convincingly of a promise. To speak kindly is to speak from the heart. It demonstrates the willingness to bring out goodness from a good heart to speak to others who seem to have evil in their hearts. Whatever is declared emerges from the inner part of the person, suggesting that it is accompanied by honesty and sincerity.

Speaking kindly to our opponents draws on various virtues or Christian qualities such as courage and humility. On the one hand, courage is needed in order to approach our opponent. We have to be emotionally strong and audacious to interact non-combatantly with the person who injured us. We would need to have put aside the desire for revenge. On the other hand, speaking kindly also suggests that the individual is displaying humility, a desirable quality. Individuals, who reach out to their perpetrators, tend to exhibit a humble attitude which requires conscientious reflection. Furthermore, they are resolute in their decisions and act from their centre of moral character. A display of attitudes such as this one echoes the inspirational view that "higher than the highest human thought can reach is God's ideal for His children. Godliness—godlikeness—is the goal to be reached."[90] Like Joseph, we can strive to reach this goal as we focus on experiencing emotional progress on our journey.

STEP 3: BE AWARE OF THE IMPACT OF CONTRASTING SPIRITUALITY

Joseph's varied experiences remind me of the distinct features between crude oil and water. When I contemplate on the features of these two liquids, I recognise that they are similar, but they also possess some differences. One difference is that, crude oil having less density, can float on water. This is to say, crude oil is lighter than water. Crude oil is a less solid substance than water, or it has a lower 'heaviness'. When we think about these two substances, water is the denser of the two liquids because it has more mass. All of these features of water are due to the atomic structure of the elements, molecules, and compounds that make it up. This illustration pinpoints a famous quote used by individuals who seek to compare and contrast characters. They often refer to the characters as being like 'oil and water'. The popular quote depicts an all-nothing or love-hate contradiction and portrays a traumatic dynamic. It illustrates a relationship at opposite ends of a pole. Emotionally, while there is no harmony, such relationships are saturated with chaos and disconnections.

The relationship between Joseph and his brothers depicted various contrasts or differences between the way they treated him and how he reacted. Joseph was an innocent favoured teenager who seemed to be happy to respond to his daddy's request, no matter how demanding, or how far it took him. His trip to the open fields where his brothers were located was surrounded with barbaric behaviour, inhumane attitudes, insensitivity and jealousy. He had entered into a dog-eat-dog world, where individuals portrayed a crab-like mentality so that they could succeed. When Joseph recognised the emotionally-destructive behaviours of his brothers while they were in the fields, confinement to his father's tent was the context in which he gained peace, protection and security.

The brothers, on seeing Joseph approaching them with a message from his father, deliberately fabricated an 'ad hoc' plan to exterminate him.[91] The repetitious use of the word 'kill' indicates intense hatred coupled with premeditated intentions. The use of such language highlights their harsh feelings for Joseph, all emanating from their envious hearts. In contrast, Joseph, on seeing his famine-stricken, guilt-ridden brothers coming to Egypt in search of food, was moved with compassion and treated them kindly. When Joseph observed his guilty brothers standing before him in the palace court, he could not succumb to a revengeful attitude, seeing that he had been travelling *on the road to forgiveness.* Individuals, who have been developing their emotional capacity to move, focus on their journey. It is such single-mindedness that contributes to us experiencing some degree of healing. At the end, we benefit by seeing emotional, psychological and spiritual progress.

The linguistic technique of contrast also appears when the brothers attempted to thwart Joseph's God-given dream. The divine interpretation revealed that his entire family would bow down to him. They made every attempt to silence the dream and by extension, to hold back a prophetic declaration from being fulfilled. Their plan to drown any memory of the dream seemed to have succeeded, but only for a short time. They had not seen Joseph for almost two decades. However, by the time the narrative reached the forty-first chapter of the Genesis narrative, Joseph's dream was revived. With Joseph being rescued from the dungeon and promoted to the position of second-in-command in Egypt, his brothers contributed to the fulfilment of the dream by bowing down to him on at least three occasions.[92] The contrast revealed the absence of fruit of the Holy Spirit and moral values which act as a guide in our spiritual journey with the Divine One.

Joseph, on stepping into Potiphar's house, immediately was surrounded by immoral acts, a lack of religious values, and vice. With Potiphar's wife chasing after him to become intimate with him, Joseph became aware of the type of people he served. The prevailing illegal sexual behaviour which accompanied the affluent lifestyle in Potiphar's house seemed to have pointed to a life lived for instant gratification. However, being imprisoned brought spiritual blessing in his life. The favour of men followed him in a positive way, with the Divine One providing providential care for him. This experience indicates the assistance Joseph gained from being incarcerated. It allowed him to be less bombarded by the issues in life, and therefore, afforded him the opportunity to find peace and safety. Such elements can contribute to one's emotional and spiritual progress.

As Joseph gained a clear view of life in Potiphar's house, it seemed to have awakened his desire to focus on developing his emotional capacity to move on emotionally and spiritually. It appeared that he used his confinement and enslavement to reframe his experiences, thereby developing the capacity to extend horizontal forgiveness to his perpetrators. Furthermore, his spirituality appeared in stark contrast to that of Potiphar's wife. Joseph, being aware of God's guiding hand every step of the way, was determined not to be part of Potiphar's wife's games and seducing activities. Thus, the use of contrast, as a literary technique, highlights the emotional and spiritual vacillation of the characters in this biblical saga. It conveys a push-pull experience which emotionally-healed individuals undergo as they seek to strive towards their divinely-imparted potential. To continue on the road to forgiveness, therefore, requires keeping focus, particularly on issues of eternal value.

SUMMARY

The development of our capacity to move on is very essential to completing the journey on the road to forgiveness. This view is more important seeing that we can experience healing on the way. It means that there is a need for us to forgive our perpetrators genuinely and wholeheartedly, and thereby, gain healing for our wounds. Furthermore, having experienced some degree of healing, the Holy Spirit aids us in reaching a place on our journey where we can display fruits of the Spirit such as kindness and love. Additionally, the Spirit embeds in us other Christian virtues such as compassion and humility, all of which aids us in striving towards our divinely-imparted potential. One's emotional capacity to move on can also be impacted upon by contrasting spirituality, where individuals with whom you interact lack Christian quality, moral values and spiritual principles. Thus, to ensure that our capacity to move on is developed well, it requires that we keep focus on the road to forgiveness which consists of various significant stages.

11
STRIVING FOR THE GOAL

Prior to the beginning of the 2012 Olympics, thousands of athletes, both seasoned and first-timers, engaged in intensive daily preparation for their sporting discipline. The Olympic Games is the world's foremost sports competition. It is the event every professional athlete dreams of attending. The Olympics begin with a number of rituals. One of these is the Olympics torch relay, which is carried through various countries around the world and finally taken through parts of the host country, leading up to the opening ceremony. Additionally, there are the parade of athletes, the raising of flags and singing of the song. The spectacular opening programme features artistic and cultural events, with the aim of awaking spectators' appetite for the varied sporting events.

The variety of training activities points to the major global sporting event. By the time the London 2012 Olympics had started, there were approximately 10,800 athletes prepared to compete. These sportsmen and women represented two hundred and four competing nations or territories. They had descended onto the Olympic Park, which comprised the Olympic Stadium and the Aquatics Centre in London, to compete for the many sought-after medals. The athletes, who resided in the Olympic Village, which was also on the site of the Olympic Park, engaged in twenty-six sports such as aquatics, athletics and gymnastics, all of which consisted of thirty-nine disciplines such as road cycling and swimming. They had competed in a total of three hundred and two sporting events. Some had reached fame and glory. Others experienced defeat! Their coaches had been inspiring them to reach their full potential. Why? Their eyes were on the gold! The athletes, representing their countries of birth or citizenship, were hungry to reach the finishing line first. This was the most important act because it was the only way they could cradle a gold medal in their hands.

A gold medal signals that you are the best in your discipline. It is a symbol of you being at the peak of your game. The gold signifies that you have performed excellently, exceptionally well or outstanding. It indicates that you are aware of what it takes to reach the highest level of your sport. The achievement of a gold medal broadcasts the message that you have reached that standard. Individuals, who acquire the gold, are seen as champions in their particular sporting discipline. Actually, every athlete dreams of standing elegantly and proudly before the judges to receive a gold cup, medal or plaque.

Although, as Christian believers, we are not striving for a temporal or earthly medal, we are involved a race which also has a goal. This type of race is seen as a marathon. It requires us to possess endurance and be persistent because we do not know when we would have completed our last lap. However, it is when the death-bell rings. It is also the time when the final trumpet sound will be heard. That will be the end of all spiritual races. Such a noise will signal the end of the race. With this in mind, what is the major essential element needed to acquire the capacity to reach the end of this 'race'? The response to this guiding question in this chapter is based on the following principle: *striving for the ultimate goal requires focusing on issues of eternal value.* This is another guiding principle which can help us reach the final stage on the road to forgiveness. However, in order to reach the end of this race, we can engage in two processes namely: (1) possess single-mindedness and (2) focus on issues of eternal value.

PROCESS ONE: POSSESS SINGLE-MINDEDNESS

In reflecting on the biblical saga of Joseph and his brothers, it appeared that Joseph was involved in an unending emotional journey. Each new eventful stage of the calamitous and stormy journey seemed to lead into a cruel and more intense ordeal than the previous one. However, a divinely orchestrated shift of events enabled Joseph's journey to reach a progressive and successful climax. So, how was he able to stay focused on his goal? How can we remain focused on our single important goal, having made progress from deep emotional pain and turmoil, great challenges and severe hardships? Importantly, it requires individuals to develop prayerfully a single-minded attitude, seasoned with the grace of God.

Individuals, in undergoing this process, need to experience a transformed heart. The twenty-first verse of the last chapter of the biblical book of Genesis demonstrates Joseph's transformed heart, out of which emerged words of assurance, hope, life and peace. Reading the scriptural account, Joseph advised his brothers: "'now therefore, do not be afraid; I will provide for you and your little ones.' And he comforted them and spoke kindly to them" (Gen 50:21). The entire emotional journey highlights the renewed character of a person who has experienced the Hand of God in his life. For instance, he had experienced divine favour (Gen 39:3, 4, 21-23), divine providence and divine protection from physical death and from a life of imprisonment. No doubt, these opportunities saddled him with the responsibility of treating his opponents with Christ-like kindness.

On experiencing some degree of healing, individuals would need to strive for the ultimate goal with single-mindedness. Insightfully, we are reminded that "the marked prosperity which attended everything placed under Joseph's care was not the result of a direct miracle; but his industry, care, and energy were crowned with the divine blessing. Joseph attributed his success to the favour of God, and even his idolatrous master accepted this as the secret of his unparalleled prosperity. Without steadfast, well-directed effort, however, success could never have been attained. God was glorified by the faithfulness of His servant. It was His purpose that in purity and uprightness the believer in God should appear in marked contrast to the worshipers of idols."[93] When we contemplate on such personal progress, there is only one action we should engage in as Joseph did, and that is, to strive for the ultimate goal.

Such a decision is based on the desire to move on from emotional hurts and difficulties. To experience this progress, it requires us to focus on our salvation and redemption which are experienced presently and are fulfilled at Christ's Second Coming. His crucifixion on the Cross has paved the way for us to become transformed in attitude, behaviour and beliefs. This Christological role of the healing Messiah has been depicted graphically:

> ⁴ Yet it was our weaknesses he carried;
>> it was our sorrows that weighed him down.
> And we thought his troubles were a punishment from God,
>> a punishment for his own sins!
> ⁵ But he was pierced for our rebellion,
>> crushed for our sins.
> He was beaten so we could be whole.
>> He was whipped so we could be healed.
> ⁶ All of us, like sheep, have strayed away.
>> We have left God's paths to follow our own.
> Yet the LORD laid on him
>> the sins of us all.
>> _____ Isaiah 53:4-6, NLT).

As part of this painful ordeal on the Cross, Christ's role involved bearing our weaknesses and sorrows (v.4), and accepting our rebellious and sinful attitudes and behaviours (v.5) so that we can be healed and ultimately be made whole. (1 Pet 2:24). The healing which Christ obtained for us has brought about a cure for our souls, and healing for our emotional pain. We can conclude that the goal of His death on the Cross was to ensure that we experienced wholeness, be reconciled to the Divine One and finally be restored fully to the original state of the human race.

We too must die while we are still alive! Have you ever thought about it? We must die daily to the sinful desires of humanity. We are also encouraged to manage our human passions, overcome the hunger for revenge, and to address the instinct to be angry always (1 Cor. 9:27). This involves putting our mind and body under strict discipline, like the athlete who is preparing for the once-in-a-lifetime Olympics race. By continuously addressing the painful issues on various levels in our life through the power of our Supreme Restorer, we gain an opportunity to reach the ultimate goal of experiencing eternal life.

BOX 11.1: THINKING ANALYTICALLY

J, a middle age educator, and mother of three, has been making every attempt to live peacefully with her female and male siblings. None of her siblings is a committed religious believer, even though they may attend religious services intermittently. Although she is at mid-life, they have been teasing her about her religious faith, engaging in name-calling, in heated arguments with her and have been objecting consistently to most of her views.

Although she resides at her own home and is single, just as some of the other siblings, she has been experiencing difficulties in getting along with them. Earlier in her life, she had been experiencing various psychological disorders such as depression. However, by attending various therapeutic-type programmes, through much prayer, fasting and bible studies, she was able to move forward emotionally. Having experienced some degree of healing, she vowed that nothing will push her back into the old emotional state. The challenges with her siblings has continued after this new experience, which she has counteracted by determining to use various resources to help her continue to move on emotionally.

The case of J above highlights a major issue, that of sibling rivalry. Evidence of this family feud is seen in the form of abuse. She has been subjected to psychological abuse in the form of name-calling, being argued with, consistently being objected to and being teased. The abuse she has experienced could have contributed to the psychological disorder of depression, possibly resulting in her being psychologically dysfunctional at the time. The fact that she is unable to get along peacefully with her siblings could suggest that there is an unresolved family issue. It could also suggest that they are jealous of her. This unhealthy family dynamic had created animosity among them, thus leading to poor interpersonal relationships. However, J has been displaying a determined spirit in an effort to remain focused. In fact, she has been using various spiritual resources to aid her in striving towards her goal of not becoming affected negatively again by the difficulties which her siblings have being posing for her.

Have you experienced healing for any of the wounds you may have been carrying? Have you made any attempt to address your spiritual illness? How important to your healing is Christ's experience from his death to his ascension? In seeking to focus on our salvation, we are encouraged to focus on our spiritual inheritance, seeing that Christ has given us the privilege of experiencing divine blessings. It is also essential that we ensure we remain in the faith by making our call and election certain (2 Peter 1:10). This also entails seeking for a new daily experience, whereby we can share with others concerning the divine power in our life.

Let us ponder further on Joseph's ordeal at this time. His reaction throughout his journey reflects his heart. In order to forgive our enemies, we need to have 'heart'. Scripture reminds us that a person can have a 'broken and a contrite heart' (Ps 51:17), an 'evil heart' (Jer. 3:17), a 'defiant and rebellious heart' (Jer. 5:23), or a 'perverse and desperately wicked heart' (Jer. 17:9). On the other hand, an individual can have a 'pure heart' (Ps.

24:4), an 'upright heart' (Ps. 32:11), a 'clean heart' (Ps. 51:10), a 'steadfast heart' (Ps 57:7) or a sincere heart (Eph 6:5). What about Joseph? His actions, attitudes, behaviour, choices and responses convey his spiritual experience. It also highlighted God's dealing with him and his willingness to strive for his goal.

When we take the time to reflect on Joseph's journey from the pit to the palace, we recognise that Joseph had a *believing heart*. Ellen G. White remarked that "Joseph's faith and integrity were to be tested by fiery trials. His master's wife endeavoured [sic] to entice the young man to transgress the law of God. Heretofore he had remained untainted by the corruption teeming in that heathen land; but this temptation, so sudden, so strong, so seductive--how should it be met? Joseph knew well what would be the consequence of resistance. On the one hand were concealment, favour [sic], and rewards; on the other, disgrace, imprisonment, perhaps death. His whole future life depended upon the decision of the moment."[94] The writer of Genesis, the first biblical book, provides us with a glimpse of Joseph's believing heart when he uncovered his identity to his brothers. During this revelation, he compared his brothers' evil motives with that of God's directive will (Gen. 45:5; 50:20a). Out of this, we observed that it was his believing heart which accounted for him experiencing the healing power of God, whereby he could engage in horizontal forgiveness and reconciliation with his deceptive brothers.

Furthermore, from our analysis of his believing heart, "Joseph's real character shines out, even in the darkness of the dungeon. He held fast his faith and patience; his years of faithful service had been most cruelly repaid, yet this did not render him morose or distrustful. He had the peace that comes from conscious innocence, and he trusted his case with God. He did not brood upon his own wrongs, but forgot his sorrow in trying to lighten the sorrows of others. He found a work to do, even in the prison."[95] This single-minded attitude also prevailed during the revelation of his identity, an experience that also enabled him to attribute his enslavement as being God's directive will for his life. Such an undertaking culminated in the rescue of at least two generations of his family of origin (Gen. 45:7-8; 50:20b). And so, it is by possessing a believing heart that we can strive for the ultimate goal, while travelling on the road to forgiveness.

Joseph also had a *humble heart*. Evidence of his humility is seen in his silence in the first four chapters of his ordeal. Imagine a person being belittled, bullied, humiliated, hunted down, jeered, mistreated and sexually abused and yet remained silent. What emotional resource could he have possessed to aid him in going through this severe testing? Author, Ellen G. White, noted that "he may think himself alone, but to every deed there is an unseen witness. The very motives of his heart are open to divine inspection. Every act, every word, every thought, is as distinctly marked as though there were only one person in the whole world, and the attention of heaven were centered [sic] upon him. Joseph suffered for his integrity, for his tempter revenged herself by accusing him of a foul crime, and causing him to be thrust into prison. Had Potiphar believed his wife's charge against Joseph, the young Hebrew would have lost his life; but the modesty and uprightness that had uniformly characterized his conduct were proof of his innocence; and yet, to save the reputation of his master's house, he was abandoned to disgrace and bondage."[96] Importantly, his humility became a driving force in him being single-minded in his dealings.

Finally, Joseph displayed an *enduring heart*. Certainly he would have been aware of his brothers' hatred towards him (Gen.37:4, 5, 8). The brothers also had undermined him by being 'cold' in their interaction with him (v.4). However, while "his [Joseph's] beautiful countenance lighted up with the Spirit of inspiration, they could not withhold their admiration; but they did not choose to renounce their evil ways, and they hated the purity that reproved their sins. The same spirit that actuated Cain was kindling in their hearts."[97] Joseph, being of a different mind set to his brothers, appeared not to be concerned about their negative attitude, even though they "could not speak peaceably to him" (Gen 37:4). Nevertheless, there was trouble rising in 'the air', to the extent that the brothers' hatred festered into envy. This led them to capture Joseph, mistreat him by throwing him into a pit and finally selling him (Gen 37:24-29). These inhumane actions have the potential to instigate a harsh retaliation in a person. They have the potential to create bitterness and hostility in the human heart, and in Joseph's. By the time he was sold as a slave to an Egyptian (Gen 37:36), we see his enduring heart emerging.

Furthermore, we see the display of his enduring heart intensifying when he was accused falsely. How could Joseph withstand being lied on by individuals with power, prestige and social status? The sacred Scriptures share the accusation: "**She** kept his cloak beside her until his master came home. Then she told him this story: 'That Hebrew slave you brought us came to me to make sport of me. But as soon as I screamed for help, he left his cloak beside me and ran out of the house.' When his master heard the story his wife told him, saying, 'This is how your slave treated me,' he burned with anger. Joseph's master took him and put him in prison, the place where the king's prisoners were confined" (Gen.39:16-19, NIV). Having been imprisoned by Potiphar and forgotten by Pharaoh's previously imprisoned chief butler, Joseph needed resources that could help him through his emotional journey. Indeed, it was his enduring heart that kept him striving for his goal. Such a resource is even more important for individuals travelling on the road to forgiveness to have an enduring heart.

PROCESS TWO: FOCUS ON ISSUES OF ETERNAL VALUE

In order to strive for the ultimate goal, it is essential that we continue to address any emotional difficulties that could hinder us from going forward. The idea of striving creates the imagery of intently stretching oneself to the limit. The nature of striving relates to reaching out into the future and extending oneself beyond the mundane, ordinary, and same-old-same-old humdrum in life. Those who desire to strive towards the ultimate goal would need to engage in the second process of focusing on issues of eternal value. An example of this process is contained in the exchange between Joseph and Potiphar's wife. This short-lived encounter became the catalyst in the plot of this biblical saga.

In charting Joseph's stormy emotional journey, Scripture provides the gritty details: "Now Joseph was well-built and handsome, and after a while his master's wife took notice of Joseph and said, 'Come to bed with me!' But he refused. 'With me in charge,' he told her, 'my master does not concern himself with anything in the house; everything he owns he has entrusted to my care. No one is greater in this house than I am. My master has withheld nothing from me except you, because you are his wife. How then could I do such a wicked thing and sin against God?' And though she spoke to Joseph day after day, he refused to go to bed with her or even be with her" (Gen. 39:6-10, NIV). Here is an example of being caught between a rock and a hard place. It is a case in which we are caught between the 'devil and the deep blue sea'. Furthermore, this experience demonstrates that Joseph "preferred to share the oppression [suffer the hardships] *and* bear the shame … rather than to have the fleeting enjoyment of a sinful life" (Heb.11:25, AMP). In essence, this erotic dialogue reveals that Joseph's heart was fixed on the goal of continuing to experience God's favour and power in his life.

From this aggressive interaction, three issues emerge. The first appears in the two dimensions of Joseph's faithfulness as a servant. Joseph was faced with being faithful to two masters, while working in Potiphar's house. The story line portrays the God of Heaven being present with and guiding Joseph at the beginning of his enslavement. However, Joseph's desire to be faithful to God's providence is intercepted vehemently by the sexual harassment of Potiphar's wife. It demonstrates the subtle workings of the evil one, but highlights the need for us to be cognizant of *God's guiding Hand on our life* before we can regulate the *demanding hand of others on our life*. Oppositely, we cannot positively experience the Hand of God on our life unless we are willing to control the hand of others on our lives. Joseph's ordeal reminds us how our demand to be faithful to those who dominate our lives and being faithful to our dreams and goals interfere with our relationship with God. We are unable to be completely faithful to earthly powers without it impacting negatively on our emotional and spiritual progress. Neither can we be careless in our connection with God without it interfering with the response to our earthly leaders. Being totally faithful to God and being completely faithful to earthly leaders are hardly inseparable

The intense pressure to remain faithful in the midst of appealing temptation bore down heavily on Joseph. The emotional and spiritual battles must have been severe. Insightfully, we are alerted that "Joseph's answer reveals the power of religious principle. He would not betray the confidence of his master on earth, and, whatever the consequences, he would be true to his Master in heaven. Under the inspecting eye of God and holy angels many take liberties of which they would not be guilty in the presence of their fellow men, but Joseph's first thought was of God."[98] To do otherwise would be to lose sight of his goal. And the result would be severely damaging and devastating. No wonder Joseph preferred to be faithful to God and maintain his emotional and spiritual progress.

The second issue emerging from the test of being faithful relates to priorities in life. When Joseph posed the rhetorical question: "How then could I do such a wicked thing and sin against God?" he was determined to keep his priorities in proper perspective. What would be his main concern? To whom would he be loyal? His God? Potiphar? Or Potiphar's wife? It all depended on where his priorities lay. A few moments of sinful pleasure would have pushed him back emotionally and spiritually. Along with this, he would have remembered the implications of Psalm 66:18, which cautions that if we hold on to lingering sins in our life and do not confess and repent of them, they would prevent the God of Heaven from listening and responding to our prayer requests.

Joseph's rhetorical question indicated that he engaged in a different type of thought process to that of Potiphar's wife. Joseph was engaged in global thinking which involves taking various issues into consideration, looking at the bigger picture, including the future outcomes, before making a decision. For example, the determined Joseph was faced with intimacy issues, displaying his masculine ego, his spiritual witness to Potiphar's household and being faithful to God. Not only was he faced with these issues, he also had to consider the impact each of them would have on his life. Having perceived the implications of all of these issues, Joseph no doubt chose to keep his spiritual witness intact. In contrast, Potiphar's wife employed sequential thinking in that her eyes were fixed on one thing – getting Joseph to commit sexual sin with her. Nothing else seemed to be important to her in spite of the ethical concerns. How did Joseph escape the attractive, luring, tantalising power of such a woman? He must have been from a special stock! Although this is a shift away from the biological nature of women's thought processes, it is the type of thought process which God would want Christians to adopt as they seek to be faithful to His teachings. Actually, global thinking aids individuals who have embarked on the road to forgiveness, in that it helps us to strive for the goal.

Such behaviours, experiences and undertakings indicate that Joseph was focusing on issues of eternal value. In fact, "God was preparing him in the school of affliction for greater usefulness, and he did not refuse the needful discipline. In the prison, witnessing the results of oppression and tyranny and the effects of crime, he learned lessons of justice, sympathy, and mercy, which prepared him to exercise power with wisdom and compassion. Joseph gradually gained the confidence of the keeper of the prison, and was finally entrusted with the charge of all the prisoners. It was the part he acted in the prison--the integrity of his daily life and his sympathy for those who were in trouble and distress--that opened the way for his future prosperity and honor [sic]. Every ray of light that we shed upon others is reflected upon ourselves. Every kind and sympathizing word spoken to the sorrowful, every act to relieve the oppressed, and every gift to the needy, if prompted by a right motive, will result in blessings to the giver."[99] When we consider Joseph's emotional journey, it appears that divine providence accompanied him every step of the way. Individuals taking the journey on the road to forgiveness need divine assistance in reaching the final stage. This implies that our emotional and spiritual progress are interdependent as we seek to focus on issues of eternal value.

The relational dynamics between Joseph and Potiphar's wife depicts how evil forces threaten our devotion to the Holy God and our spirituality. This is the third issue arising out of this narrative involving Joseph and Potiphar's wife. In particular, it highlights the persistence of the evil one who engineers a fierce and heated battle against individuals who seek to strive for the ultimate goal of experiencing the eternal blessing of everlasting life. Also, this dynamic elicits the need for spiritual integrity. This one-off scene of sexual harassment was an opportunity to refine Joseph's spiritual integrity. He had to be emotionally strong, seeing that his eyes were on the goal. His desire was to focus on his eternal fate. The statement "she kept putting pressure on Joseph day after day" (Gen 39:10, NLT), suggests that the advances from Potiphar's wife had developed gradually. Maybe she drew close by now and again, pretending to inspect his work. But in reality, she wanted to get a clue about the type of spices he wore (there was no Chanel No. 5 in ancient biblical times)! Maybe she rested her hand on his shoulder as a prop, pretending to fix her shoe strap. The time bomb was ticking. The gigantic avalanche was approaching the tightly bolted door of integrity. What the world of Potiphar's wife had to offer was contrary to Joseph's moral compass. He saw her for whom she truly was – crafty, devious, greedy, jealous, seductive and sensual. In fact, it is an essential value that is worth adopting by those who seek to experience progress on an emotional, psychological or spiritual level.

SUMMARY

The guiding principle of this chapter indicates that *striving for the ultimate goal requires us to focus on issues of eternal value.* This can be achieved by engaging in two processes, one of which is to possess a single-minded attitude during our emotional journey. One way by which this can be achieved is by developing a believing, enduring and humble heart. It is such a heart that motivates God to intervene on our behalf because He reads our motives. Second, it is important to focus on issues which point to eternity. Being faithful to the God of Heaven, setting our priorities in life in the right place and being aware of the threat and persistence of evil forces around us are ways by which we can remain focus on issues with eternal significance.

A FINAL THOUGHT
PROMOTING SPIRITUAL ESTEEM

We began this journey *On the Road to Forgiveness* by discussing the need to promote one's emotional wellbeing through the use of psychological and spiritual resources. In particular, a religious practice which can be beneficial to promoting our wellbeing is building *spiritual esteem*. The concept, spiritual esteem, refers to the degree of confidence (faith) a mature believer displays in her daily Christian life. It involves developing a strong relationship with God and believing firmly that Christ has saved her and can empower her through the indwelling of the Holy Spirit. Building a spiritual esteem can occur when we engage continually in spiritual disciplines in order to develop our spiritual relationship with Christ. Some of these spiritual disciplines are bible studies, intercessory prayer, and theological reflection, appropriately suited to building a high spiritual esteem.

How does spiritual esteem relate to horizontal forgiveness? Scholars advocate that forgiveness is both a religious practice and a psychological construct.[100] From a religious perspective, it is extended on intra- and inter-personal levels. On the other hand, from a psychological point of view, it is conceptualised on state and trait levels. The concept also implies that there is theological input and is based on a high level of spiritual maturity which contribute to a person engaging in the act of interpersonal forgiveness.

Throughout this book I have advocated simultaneously two important areas: psychology and spirituality. I seek to apply psychological theory to the establishment of spiritual esteem, and demonstrate the importance of spirituality to this aspect of our life. Additionally, I attempt to underpin the thesis of the book by reflecting Adventist health and theological perspectives within the context of practising forgiveness.

Individuals, who seek to develop a high spiritual esteem, tend to address various the psychological issues important for extending horizontal forgiveness. Divine assurance through the Sacred Scriptures assists such individuals in feeling a sense of belonging and being loved, all of which help victims and perpetrators to feel accepted. Evidence of this is seen in Romans 8:15-17 which points out that individuals who commit their lives to the Infinite Holy God are seen as His obedient children, and are given the right to be inheritors of all of His blessings. Furthermore, having been considered God's children, He extends unconditional love to such individuals (1 John 3.1). Additionally, this assurance contributes to the high value and great worth individuals put on their relationship with Christ, the Redeemer. By developing a high spiritual esteem various psychological needs are met, thus providing a better emotional and spiritual position from which to offer forgiveness to others.

Seeing that forgiveness is a religious practice, considering one's spirituality is important because it is this aspect of one's life that provides the capacity to extend forgiveness. However, our spirituality deepens on knowing that we "were washed clean (purified by a complete atonement for sin and made free from the guilt of sin), and [you] were consecrated (set apart, hallowed), and [you] were justified [pronounced righteous, by trusting] in the name of the Lord Jesus Christ and in the [Holy] Spirit of our God" (1 Cor. 6:11, AMP). This spiritual cleansing brings about a renewed and transformed life, all of which contribute to the development of one's spiritual esteem. Individuals experiencing such a spiritual progress cannot help but be compassionate to hurting individuals or perpetrators and ultimately forgive them.

Spiritual esteem is built on the Christological input through the sacrifice on Calvary's Cross. Our relationship with God is enhanced when we "... spend a thoughtful hour each day in contemplation of the life of Christ. We should take it point by point, and let the imagination grasp each scene, especially the closing ones. As we thus dwell upon His great sacrifice for us, our confidence in Him will be more constant, our love will be quickened,

189

and we shall be more deeply imbued with His spirit. If we would be saved at last, we must learn the lesson of penitence and humiliation at the foot of the cross."[101] It is Christ who set the example for us to follow in all aspects of our daily life, including extending forgiveness to others. This theological perspective contributes to the improvement of our spirituality, through which our spiritual esteem is developed further.

Developing a high spiritual esteem requires us to display qualities such as humility, honesty, openness and safe vulnerability. A demonstration of such Christian qualities call for commitment and sacrifice. They call for sacrifice of individuality, our opinions, our priorities, personal desires and self-pleasure. It is no wonder that some individuals are unable to reach the stage of being willing to forgive because they seem to have a low spiritual esteem. May the Divine One guide you *on the road to forgiveness* and enable you to experience healing on the way!

APPENDICES

APPENDIX A

DISCUSSION GUIDE

Having read and reflected on the content of the previous chapters, take some time to engage in the study below for *group discussion* or at your leisure for *individual reflection*.

Introduction

1. What is your personal definition of forgiveness?

....

....

....

....

2. Compare the four definitions of forgiveness and identify the similarities.

....

....

....

....

3. After prayerfully study Philippians 3:7-9, identify the words which are repeated often? Why do you think these words are repeated so often?

....

....

....

....

4. Review the three dimensions of forgiveness. Which of these dimensions pose the most difficulty for you? How do you overcome this difficulty?

....

....

....

....

5. Review the major principle of this volume on page xxxiii. How would you determine whether or not you are ready to forgive an individual?

....

....

....

....

<u>Chapter 1</u>

FACING THE PAINFUL MOMENT

1. Share two spiritual resources that can aid you in promoting emotional wellbeing?

....
....
....
....

2. How can you apply the message in John 6:63 to your personal bible study sessions?

....
....
....
....

3. If you were struggling emotionally, share one way by which you would seek to develop your emotional wellbeing.

....
....
....
....

4. Record Psalm 119:105 on the lines below, memorise it and then write out one insight or message you have gathered from the text.

....
....
....
....

5. What unpleasant past painful and unresolved issues (baggage) do you have? How are they impacting on you emotionally, psychologically or spiritually?

....

....

....

....

Chapter 2

THE IMPACT OF UNSURRENDERED PAINFUL ISSUES

1. Which needs on Maslow's Hierarchy are you seeking to meet at this time in your life? How would these needs assist your emotional and spiritual progress?

....
....
....
....

2. Explain in your own words how hurting individuals seek to avoid focusing on painful emotional issues.

....
....
....
....

3. How does Galatians 5:19-20 relate to our unwillingness to surrender our angry, bitter and hostile attitude?

....
....
....
....

4. Prayerfully read Mt 6:14-15. How does this text relate to our emotional and spiritual progress?

....
....
....
....

5. What do you think is the significance of repeating the word 'forgive' in Mt 6:14-15?

....

....

....

....

<u>Chapter 3</u>

RELEASING THE PRESSURE VALVE

1. In your own words define *reframe*.

....
....
....
....

2. Why is it important to reframe your problems in light of the need to forgive?

....
....
....
....

3. Prayerfully study Philippians 3:7-9. How can our focus on Christ assist us with our past painful unresolved issues?

....
....
....
....

4. Read Phil 3:8. Write it out in the space below. How would the different aspects of Christ's life in this text help us in relation to our past unpleasant lifestyle?

....
....
....
....

5. What do you understand by the term 'safe vulnerability'? How important are qualities such as boldness and empathy to our emotional healing?

....

....

....

....

<u>Chapter 4</u>

EXPLORING THE MIND

1. Which level of consciousness regulates unpleasant experiences in order that they do not surface into the conscious region of the mind? Why is this necessary?

....

....

....

....

2. Describe a time when an unpleasant issue that you had buried resurfaced into your consciousness. How did you address this situation?

....

....

....

....

3. Share one similarity between the conscious and the preconscious sections of the mind. What emotional/psychological advantage does this have for us?

....

....

....

4. Read 2 Tim 1:7 and compare it with Romans 12:1-2. How does having a sound mind contribute to our personal transformation and restoration?

....

....

....

....

5. Review Romans 12:2. How does having a renewed mind help us relate to others?

....

....

....

....

<u>Chapter 5</u>

THE BATTLE IS IN THE MIND

1. Share two types of defence mechanisms that adults tend to use to avoid/ escape painful issues?

....
....
....
....

2. Study Romans 7:21- 25. How can the conflict between the law and the flesh affect our spirituality?

....
....
....
....

3. Prayerfully reflect on Col 3:2. How can fixing our minds on spiritual issues contribute to our healing?

....
....
....
....

4. Identify an individual with whom you have been experiencing interpersonal problems? How would expressing the agape love towards this person help the relationship between both of you?

....
....
....
....

5. Having read up to Chapter 5 of this volume, how has these chapters helped you so far? Discuss any changes that the Holy Spirit is guiding you to make?

....

....

....

....

<u>Chapter 6</u>

LEAVE YOUR PAINFUL PAST IN THE PAST

1. State two (2) types of wounded-ness. After reading this chapter, take the Inventory on Emotional Wounded-ness. See Appendix C. Identify your degree of wounded-ness and share how it is impacting (has impacted) on you.

....
....
....
....

2. Reflect on 2 Corinthians 5:17. Compare it with Romans 6:6. What are the similarities in the two verses? How can these verses assist us in looking to the future as opposed to living in the past?

....
....
....
....

3. Share two (2) goals you would like to set for yourself to assist you in leaving the difficult 'past' in the past.

....
....
....
....

4. Explain the term 'single-mindedness'. To what extent do you have the ability to be single-minded in seeking to experience emotional progress?

....
....
....

5. How has this chapter helped you in your journey towards forgiveness?

....

....

....

....

....

Chapter 7

FORGIVENESS – A HEALING FACTOR

1. After reading the first perspective on **Pages 109-112,** discuss the relationship between physical and spiritual illness.

....
....
....
....

2. Share two ways in which forgiveness helps with restoration of emotional health.

....
....
....
....

3. How does religious practices impact one's ability to extend forgiveness?

....
....
....
....

4. How does extending forgiveness help with emotional freedom?

....
....
....
....

5. Discuss the relationship between forgiveness and healing.

....
....
....
....

<u>Chapter 8</u>

PSYCHOLOGICAL BENEFITS OF FORGIVENESS

1. State two (2) ways by which the re-appraisal of our attitudes and behaviours can impact on our psychological wellbeing.

....
....
....
....

2. Read Colossians 3:8. How does this verse contribute to the instructions found in Proverbs 15:18?

....
....
....
....

3. Discuss two emotional issues which highlight that a person may be psychologically dysfunctional.

....
....
....
....

4. Discuss three ways by which forgiveness is related to reconciliation.

....
....
....
....

5. Study prayerfully 2 Corinthians 5:18-20. Explain how psychological components such as open-mindedness, trust and truthfulness contributes to the process of reconciliation.

....

....

....

....

<u>Chapter 9</u>

EXPERIENCING EMOTIONAL AND SPIRITUAL HEALING

1. Identify two (2) ways in which the needs for affiliation (N Aff) can impact positively on our emotional wellbeing.

....
....
....
....

2. Discuss how the need for affiliation is related to our degree of wounded-ness. Refer to Figure 6.2 in Chapter Six.

....
....
....
....

3. Explain what minimal effective responses (MERs) are, and discuss how they can contribute to progress in one's emotional health.

....
....
....
....

4. How can a person, who has experienced emotional and spiritual healing, display 'safe vulnerability?

....
....
....
....

5. Discuss two ways by which fear can affect the healing process for emotionally-wounded individuals.

....

....

....

....

Chapter 10

DEVELOPING YOUR EMOTIONAL CAPACITY TO MOVE ON

1. In your own words state what is involved in providing 'optimal forgiveness'.

....
....
....
....

2. List three (3) processes that can help individuals reach their God-given potential.

....
....
....
....

3. How does forgiving someone impact on our psychological needs?

....
....
....
....

4. How does forgiveness relate to the harmony in relationships?

....
....
....
....

5. How does guilt affect our ability to forgive others?

....
....
....
....

Chapter 11

STRIVING FOR THE GOAL

1. What do you understand by the term 'single-mindedness?

....
....
....
....

2. What is the relationship between a contrite heart and making emotional progress?

....
....
....
....

3. Study Ezekiel 36:24-28. How can we acquire an obedient heart so that we can engage in horizontal forgiveness?

....
....
....
....

4. Discuss the effects of a 'believing' heart, a 'humble' heart and an 'enduring' heart on our emotional and spiritual healing.

....
....
....
....

5. Discus any three areas which a person focuses on when he/she is concerned about issues of eternal value.

....

....

....

....

APPENDIX B

A PSYCHO-SPIRITUAL APPROACH TO THE INTERDEPENDENCE BETWEEN FORGIVENESS AND HEALING

In exploring the topic of horizontal forgiveness, this volume attempted to address the principal question: How can individuals gain emotional freedom from their painful past issues which negatively impact their daily lives? I also hold the view that hurting individuals, in continuously carrying unresolved past painful issues, experience difficulties with interpersonal/ horizontal forgiveness and therefore, are unable to progress emotionally and spiritually. Additionally, the major principle on which this volume is based, states that in order *to forgive, a person needs to experience some degree of healing; and to experience healing, an individual needs to forgive themselves and others.* Chapters seven and nine of this book explore the two sub-sections of the above-mentioned major principle. However, in order to illustrate the principle pictorially, the model seen below has been designed to provide a visual representation of the psycho-spiritual approach adopted in this volume in relation to the interdependence of experiencing healing and extending forgiveness.

From the diagram, the model consists of two processes: experiencing healing and extending forgiveness, the central and motivating element, that being Christ-the Healing Redeemer and the triangle which represents the base or foundation of the model. Placing the two processes at the top of the model reveals a direct proportion between them, in that, high or wholehearted forgiveness can bring about an assured degree of healing. Also there exists an inter-relationship among these four elements, all connected by the central element.

The two sets of bi-directional arrows indicate the interdependence, and link between healing and forgiveness, where experiencing a measure of healing aids in the extension of forgiveness. Conversely, extending forgiveness to oneself or another person assists in bring about healing. The bold printed arrows indicate the permanence, to the extent, that whenever there is some degree of emotional, psychological or spiritual wounded-ness, both forgiveness and healing are necessary and must take place in order for individuals to move forward. The light-printed single arrows indicate that it is through Christ, the Compassionate Redeemer of the human race, that individuals acquire the capacity to forgive. Furthermore, Christ is the one who also brings about the healing, and therefore, becomes central to the interdependent relationship between forgiveness and healing.

The bold single arrow denotes the fact that Christ inspires and equips individuals to engage in various religious practices such as bible studies, fasting and intercessory prayer and also to use other resources such as counselling. These psychological and spiritual resources are contained in the triangle which acts as the base and impacts on individuals' capacity to extend forgiveness and experience healing.

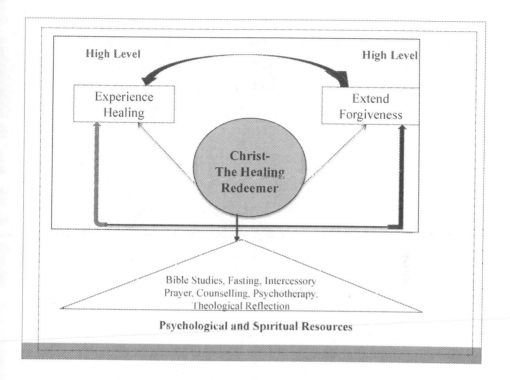

A Psycho-spiritual Approach to the Interdependence of Forgiveness and Healing

Emotional health fluctuates, seeing that individuals interact with each other with a high probability of being wounded. With this being a reality in human daily life experiences, the model is advantageous, in that, it is cyclic in nature because of the constant need to engage in the processes such as extending forgiveness at different unpredictable times in our lives. Furthermore, the cyclic feature of the model fits with the interdependence between healing and forgiveness, to the point that, the third and central aspect of the model, that being Christ, impacts on these two other aspects of the model.

There is evidence of the pre-supposition that the target audience of this volume adopts a Christian worldview and concurs with a Christian theology. Such a profound limitation of this model could negatively affect its application to the resolution of emotional difficulties by adherents of non-Christian faiths. Although, various elements of the model are parallel with other religious traditions such as Islam and Judaism, some non-Western religions may not perceive their deity as being central to the interdependence between forgiveness and healing.

A further limitation is that the model omits the physiological aspect of healing and forgiveness. This view is taken since people who contend with issues relating to forgiveness undergo physiological changes such as heart rate and blood pressures.[102] Although few studies are available to support the perspective that forgiveness is associated positively with physical health, there are nevertheless, benefits. Additionally, individuals with certain emotionally-related physical illnesses, could experience physical healing when emotional difficulties are resolved appropriately.[103] For example, individuals suffering from unexplained neck pains could be experiencing negative stress. In addition, when individuals adopt a forgiving attitude, such individuals tend to adopt health promoting behaviours such as engaging in better self-care. Thus, it is acknowledged that the physical dimension of these two interdependent concepts is invisible in the model.

APPENDIX C

DEGREE OF EMOTIONAL WOUNDEDNESS

Individuals at some time in their life will be affected emotionally, physically, psychologically or spiritually. Depending on the seriousness of the impact, such individuals could be left in pain. People who have been injured tend to experience pain at different degrees, be it being bruised or damaged. In order to assess the severity of your level of wounded-ness, this inventory has been designed to provide a gauge of your level of wounded-ness. In the event that your score indicates a moderate to severe/profound degree of wounded-ness, it would be advantageous to see a psychotherapist or counselling practitioner.

****

Calculating Your Score

Instructions: After completing each category of emotional wounded-ness, count the number of ticks for each rating in each column and place them on the dotted lines in brackets. Afterwards, multiply the number in the brackets and then ADD all sub-totals to arrive at a **FINAL TOTAL** for each category of emotional wounded-ness. Afterwards, tick the scoring range in the chart placed in SECTION B, below on **Page** into which your final total fit.

EXAMPLE: 0 +   3 +   4 +   6 +   4 = 17
                    (0 x 2) + (1x3) + (2x2) + (3x2) + (4x1) =

This score of 17 falls in the second category of partially wounded-ness in the chart above.

YOUR SCORES:

Emotionally Damaged: **(0 x …) + (1 x…) + (2 x…) + (3 x…) + (4 x….) =**

LEVEL 1 (Part A)

Identifying Degrees of Emotional Wounded-ness

Examine the Inventory below which describes each degree of wounded-ness. Please give a score to each **statement based on your interactions with others one month or more ago.** Use the space labelled 'Other Issues' at the bottom of the grid to add items you want to include for your own reference.

0-Not At All	1-Sometimes	2-Moderately	3-Very Much		4-Definitely				
					RATINGS				
LEVEL 1					0	1	2	3	4
1. There are no unresolved issues from the past or that are present in my life now.									
2. My emotional level is excellent and I am at an emotional peak.									
3. My emotional health is restored fully and I am focusing on being who I ought to be.									
4. I am at peace with myself and others.									
5. I do not have any emotional pain, hurts or injuries.									
6. There is an inner sense of oneness and total unity with myself, the Divine Being and others									
7. I am truly happy, emotionally fulfilled and emotionally Satisfied									
8. There is no one with whom I need to reconcile presently.									
9. I have been facing the difficult issues in my life and discussing the problems with the person(s) involved.									
10. In rating my degree of emotional wellness out of ten, with ten being emotionally whole, I would rate myself at 9 or 10.									
Other Issues									
Total for each column									

YOUR SCORE IN THIS CATEGORY:

Level 1: $(0 \text{ x } ...) + (1 \text{ x} ...) + (2 \text{ x} ...) + (3 \text{ x} ...) + (4 \text{ x} ....) =$

LEVEL 2 (Part A)

Identifying Degrees of Emotional Wounded-ness

Examine the Inventory below which describes each degree of wounded-ness. Please score each **statement based on your interactions with others one month or more ago.** Use the space labelled 'Other Issues' at the bottom of the grid to add items you want to include for your own reference.

0-Not At All	1-Sometimes	2-Moderately	3-Very Much		4-Definitely				
					RATINGS				
LEVEL 2					0	1	2	3	4
1. I find it difficult sometimes to get through the day emotionally.									
2. I have slight emotional pain and hurts from the past.									
3. I tend to be slightly moody and emotionally tired due to my emotional pain and hurts.									
4. I protect myself by being angry with others.									
5. Most of the time I am in a defensive mode during my daily encounter with the world.									
6. Most of the time I hide or withdraw and sometimes pretend that I do not care about people, but in reality, I do.									
7. I am experiencing a situation which has slightly dented my feelings.									
8. Various interactions with other people in the past have put a dent on and negatively impacted my ego.									
9. I am recovering from past hurtful issues.									
10. In rating my degree of emotional wellness out of ten, with ten being emotionally whole, I would rate myself at 7 or 8.									
Other Issues									
Total for each column									

YOUR SCORE IN THIS CATEGORY:

Level 2: $(0 \times \ldots) + (1 \times \ldots) + (2 \times \ldots) + (3 \times \ldots) + (4 \times \ldots) =$

LEVEL 3 (Part A)

Identifying Degrees of Emotional Wounded-ness

Examine the Inventory below which describes each degree of wounded-ness. Please give a score to each **statement based on your interactions with others one month or more ago.** Use the space labelled 'Other Issues' at the bottom of the grid to add items you want to include for your own reference.

0-Not At All	1-Sometimes	2-Moderately	3-Very Much		4-Definitely				
					RATINGS				
LEVEL 3					**0**	**1**	**2**	**3**	**4**
1. I am over-sensitive to factors that did not bother me previously.									
2. There is a sense of inner emotional pain and hurt that does not seem to go away.									
3. I become irritable with others, even if they are not doing anything undesirable.									
4. My tolerance level with others is low, in that, I expect and demand a lot from them.									
5. I I find it easy to lash out or display sudden outbursts of anger, hatred and resentment. These emotions 'rise up' within me at the slightest offense from others.									
6. It is very difficult, if not impossible, to love and therefore, forgive others, myself or the Divine Being.									
7. It is difficult to perceive and recognise clearly the love of others and of the Divine Being in my life. I also find it difficult to receive love, and therefore I put up an emotional 'wall' which prevents the flow of love into my life.									
8. I find myself blaming the Divine Being for my troubles and Hardships. My unresolved painful situation makes me feel hostile towards others, the Divine Being and myself. This leads to bitterness developing in my heart.									

9. I am driven to find happiness, meaning and purpose by achieving college degrees, a career promotion, and financial success among other things. I pursue things which I think will create lasting happiness and purpose to my life.					
10. In rating my degree of emotional wellness out of ten, with ten being emotionally whole, I would rate myself at 5 or 6.					
Other Issues					
Total for each column					

YOUR SCORE IN THIS CATEGORY:

Level 3: $(0 \text{ x } ...) + (1 \text{ x}...) + (2 \text{ x}...) + (3 \text{ x}...) + (4 \text{ x}....) =$

LEVEL 4 (Part A)

Identifying Degrees of Emotional Wounded-ness

Examine the Inventory below which describes each degree of wounded-ness. Please give a score to each **statement based on your interactions with others one month or more ago.** Use the space labelled 'Other Issues' at the bottom of the grid to add items you want to include for your own reference.

0-Not At All	1-Sometimes	2-Moderately	3-Very Much			4-Definitely		
						RATINGS		
LEVEL 4				**0**	**1**	**2**	**3**	**4**
1. I do not have the emotional capacity or physical ability to perform various daily tasks.								
2. Most times I feel depressed, lonely and stressed.								
3. Most times I want to cry and I have lost my self-confidence.								
4. I have lost the ability to get back on track with and control my life.								
5. I feel helpless and fearful about everything.								
6. The thoughts of being emotionally broken constantly runs Through my mind.								
7. I lack the emotional strength to forgive those who have hurt me.								
8. I lack self-esteem and do not see myself as good as others because I am useless.								
9. I am frequently distressed to the point of being physically ill								
10. In rating my degree of emotional wellness out of ten, with ten being emotionally whole, I would rate myself at 3 or 4.								
Other Issues								
Total for each column								

YOUR SCORE IN THIS CATEGORY:

Level 4: $(0 \text{ x } \ldots) + (1 \text{ x} \ldots) + (2 \text{ x} \ldots) + (3 \text{ x} \ldots) + (4 \text{ x} \ldots) =$

LEVEL 5 (Part A)

Identifying Degrees of Emotional Wounded-ness

Examine the Inventory below which describes each degree of wounded-ness. Please give a score to each **statement based on your interactions with others one month or more ago.** Use the space labelled 'Other Issues' at the bottom of the grid to add items you want to include for your own reference.

0-Not At All	1-Sometimes	2-Moderately	3-Very Much		4-Definitely			
					RATINGS			
LEVEL 5				0	1	2	3	4
1. My sense of security has been shattered deeply.								
2. I feel very anxious, and afraid most times. Also I feel helpless, hopeless and very vulnerable. This makes me feel very sad and therefore engage in self-blame frequently.								
3. I am overwhelmed with a number of difficult circumstances This leads to a sense of loneliness in my life.								
4. I am confused and find it difficult to concentrate.								
5. I withdraw and totally avoid contact with other people								
6. On a number of occasions, I experience terrifying memories, nightmares or flashbacks about the emotionally- difficult situations from the past.								
7. I avoid more and more things and situations that remind me of the traumatic situation which I experienced previously								
8. I experience fatigue, have severe muscle tension, and am emotionally numb, which cause me to be disconnected from other people.								
9. My emotional state leads me to use alcohol or other harmful drugs to make me feel better.								

10. In rating my degree of emotional wellness out of ten, with ten being emotionally whole, I would rate myself at 1 or 2.					
Other Issues					
Total for each column					

YOUR SCORE IN THIS CATEGORY:

Level 5: $(0 \times \ldots) + (1 \times \ldots) + (2 \times \ldots) + (3 \times \ldots) + (4 \times \ldots) =$

Part B
Indicating and Analysing the Score

Category of Emotional Wounded-ness	Scores			
	0 – 10	11 – 20	21 - 30	31 – 40
	Degree of Emotional Wounded-ness			
	Mildly	Partially	Moderately	Extremely
Whole				
Bruised				
Wounded				
Broken				
Damaged				

EXAMPLE: 0 +   3 +   4 +   6 +   4 = 17

(0 x 2 +   (1x3) +   (2x2) +   (3x2) +   (4x1) =

This score of 17 falls in the second category of partially wounded-ness in the chart above.

Profile on Degree of Emotional Wounded-ness		
Category of Emotional Wounded-ness	Total Score	Degree of Wounded-ness
Level 1 (Whole)		
Level 2 (Bruised)		
Level 3 (Wounded)		
Level 4 (Broken)		
Level 5 (Damaged)		

NB: The category with the highest score is your degree of emotional wounded-ness

END NOTES

1   Gary R. Collins, *Christian Counseling: A Comprehensive Guide* (Dallas, TX: Word Publishing, rev. edn, 1988), p. 130.

2   Everett L. Worthington Jr., *Hope-focused Marriage Counselling: A Guide to Brief Therapy* (Downers Grove, IL: InterVarsity Press, 1999, p. 130.

3   In *Set the Captives Free: Experiencing Healing through Holistic Restoration* (Bloomington, IN: AuthorHouse, 2013), I have designed the Holistic Restoration Programme. On pages 30-33, I have shared the elements of the hierarchy and explained how it operates. A full description and discussion on the entire hierarchy can be found in *Set the Captives Free: Experiencing Victory in Emotional Warfare (In Press)*.

4   This principle has been shared initially in my volume, *Set the Captives Free: 12 Studies for Groups or Individuals (*Bloomington, IN: AuthorHouse, 2013), p.55.

5   P. LeFrevre, "Prayer", in R.J. Hunter (ed.), *Dictionary of Pastoral Care and Counselling* (Nashville TN: Abingdon Press, 1990), pp. 937-938.

6   W. L. Liefeld,, 'Prayer' in G. W. Bromiley, R. K. Harrison and W. S. Lasor (eds), *The International Standard Bible Encyclopedia 3* (Grand Rapids MI: Eerdmans, 1986), p.939.

7   In my volume, *I Felt the Hand of God: A Gripping Story of a Shattered Dream,* (Seattle, WA: CreateSpace, 2007 pp. 140-142, I shared the secrets of my personal spiritual victory, and identified prayer as an important resource.

8   Mark R. McMinn, *Psychology, Theology and Spirituality in Christian Counseling,*(Wheaton, IL: Tyndale House Publishers, Inc., 1996), p. 76.

9   Marshall, *I Felt the Hand of God,* p. 141.

10   Ellen G. White, *Steps to Christ*, (Mountain View, CA: Pacific Press, 1892), p.93.

11   Ellen G. White, *Messages to Young People* (Washington, D.C: Review & Herald Pub. Assn., 1930), p. 253.

12   White, *Messages to Young People*, p. 255.

13   Robert L. Kinast, *Let Ministry Teach: A Guide to Theological Reflection* (Collegeville, MN: Liturgical Press, 1996), pp. viii, x.

14   Fritz Guy, *Thinking Theologically: Adventist Christianity and the Interpretation of Faith* (Berrien Springs, MI: Andrews University Press, 1999), p.49.

15   Guy, *Thinking Theologically*, p. 135.

16   Richard Nelson-Jones, *Theory and Practice of Counselling and Therapy*, (London: SAGE, 2001, 3rd edn), p.2.

17   Siang-Yang Tan, *Counseling and Psychotherapy: A Christian Perspective* (Grand Rapids, MI: Baker Academic, 2011), pp. 1-2.

18   Gretchen Reevy, Yvette Malamud Ozer, and Yuri Ito, *Encyclopaedia of Emotion,* Vol. 1 (Santa Barbara, CA: Greenwood/ABC-CLIO, LLC, 2010), p. 186.

19   Ellen G. White, *Story of Redemption* (Hagerstown, MD: Review and Herald Publishing Association, 1947), p. 268.

20   John T. Squires, "Acts" in James D. G. Dunn and John W. Rogerson (eds), *Commentary on the Bible* (Grand Rapids, MI: Eerdmans, 2003), pp. 1213-1267 (1258).

21   McMinn, *Psychology, Theology and Spirituality in Christian Counseling*, p.216.

22   Ellen G. White, *Thoughts from the Mount of Blessings* (Mountain View, CA: Pacific Press Publishing Association, 1896), p. 130.

23   Ellen G. White, *The Acts of the Apostles* (Mountain View, CA: Pacific Press Publishing Association, 1941), p.126.

24   This story is an abridged version of the full version shared in my volume, *A Journey of the Bold and the Young: Living on the Edge* (Milton Keynes, Buckinghamshire, UK: AuthorHouse, 2010), pp. 1-2.

25   Reevy et al., *Encyclopedia of Emotion,* Vol. 1, p. 192.

26 World Health Organisation, *The ICD-10 Classification of Mental and Behavioural Disorders: Clinical Descriptions and Diagnostic Guidelines* (Geneva: WHO, 1992), p. 119

27 E. G. White, *Selected Messages,* Vol. 2, (Mountain View, CA: Pacific Press Publishing Association, 1958), p.523.

28 Everett L Worthington Jr., Jack W Berry and Les Parrott III, 'Unforgiveness, Forgiveness, Religion, and Health' in Thomas G. Plante and Allen C. Sherman (eds) *Faith and Health: Psychological Perspective* (NY: The Guilford Press, 2001), pp. 107-138 (108).

29 Alex H. S. Harris & Carl E. Thoresen, "Forgiveness, Un-forgiveness, Health, and Disease" in Everett L. Worthington, Jr. (ed), *Handbook of Forgiveness* (East Sussex: Routledge, 2005), pp.321-333 (322,324).

30 Ellen G. White, *Christ Object Lessons* (Washington, D.C: Review And Herald Publishing Assn., 1923), p.251.

31 White, *Christ Object Lessons*, p. 251. Italics added.

32 White, *Thoughts from the Mount of Blessings*, p. 56.

33 Mary-Joan Gerson, *The Embedded Self: An Integrative Psychodynamic and Systemic Perspective on Couples and Family Therapy* (East Sussex: Routledge, 2nd edn, 2010), p. 195.

34 M. G. Fox, 'Reframe' in Irving B. Weiner and W. Edward Craighead (eds), *The Corsini Encyclopedia of Psychology,* Volume 4, (Hoboken, NJ: John Wiley & Sons, 2010), pp.1442-1444 (1443).

35 White, *Thoughts from the Mount of Blessings*, p. 129.

36 See R. Gross and R. McIlveen, *Psychology: A New Introduction* (London: Hodder & Stoughton, 1998), p. 166, for a discussion on different types of coping strategies.

37 Ellen G. White, *Testimonies for the Church,* Vol. 1, (Mountain View, CA: Pacific Press Publishing Association, 1948), p.346.

38 See Worthington, *Hope-focused Marriage Counselling*, p. 130 for his definition of empathy; In Martin L. Hoffman, *Empathy and Moral Development: Implications for*

Caring and Justice (Cambridge: Cambridge University Press, 2001), pp. 4-5, the author discusses his perspective of the two-fold nature of empathy.

[39] Emanuele Castano, 'Antisocial Behaviour in Individuals and Groups: An Empathy-focused Approach' in Kay Deaux and Mark Snyder (eds), *The Oxford Handbook of Personality and Social Psychology* (Oxford University Press, 2012), pp.419-445 (422).

[40] Drew Westen, Joel Weinberger and Rebekah Bradley, 'Motivation, Decision-making and Consciousness: From Psychodynamic to Subliminal Priming and Emotional Constraint Satisfaction' in Philip David Zelazo, Morris Moscovitch, and Evan Thompson (eds), *The Cambridge Handbook of Consciousness* (NY: University press, 2007), pp. 673-702 (676).

[41] Ellen G. White, *Fundamentals of Education,* (Mountain View, CA: Pacific Press Publishing Association, 1923), *p.*426.

[42] Ellen G. White, *Testimonies for the Church*, Vol. 5 (Mountain View, CA: Pacific Press Publishing Association, 1882), p. 111.

[43] Wilma Bucci, *Psychoanalysis and Cognitive Science: A Multiple Code Theory* (NY: Guilford Press, 1997), p. 28; Jean Laplanche and Jean-Bertrand Pontalis, *The Language of Psychoanalysis*, (London: Hogarth Press, 1973), p. 326.

[44] Raymond J. Corsini (ed.), *The Dictionary of Psychology* (London: Brunner-Routledge, 2002), p.757.

[45] Corsini, *The Dictionary of Psychology*, p. 871.

[46] Eric Rassin, *Thought Suppression* (Oxford: Elsevier Ltd, 2005), p.13.

[47] Ellen G. White, *Testimonies for the Church*, Vol. 3 (Mountain View, CA: Pacific Press Publishing Association, 1872), p.184.

[48] Ellen G. White, *The Ministry of Healing* (Mountain View, CA: Pacific Press,1942), p.241.

[49] Willem S. Prinsloo, 'The Psalms' in James D. G. Dunn and John W. Rogerson (eds), *Commentary on the Bible*, (Grand Rapids, MI: Eerdmans, 2003), pp. 364-436 (422).

[50] Prinsloo, 'The Psalms', p. 422.

[51] Ibid.

52 Charles A. Wanamaker, 'Philippians' in James D. G. Dunn and John W. Rogerson (eds), *Commentary on the Bible*, (Grand Rapids, MI: Eerdmans, 2003), pp. 1394-1403 (1400).

53 Wanamaker, 'Philippians', p. 1400.

54 McMinn, *Psychology, Theology and Spirituality in Christian Counseling*, p.210

55 White, *The Ministry of Healing*, p.77.

56 See a full discussion of this perspective in Craig A. Evans, 'Mark' in James D. G. Dunn and John W. Rogerson (eds), *Commentary on the Bible*, (Grand Rapids, MI: Eerdmans, 2003), pp. 1064-1105 (1071).

57 Nicholas T. Wright, *Mark for Everyone* (London: SPCK, 2004), p. 18.

58 White, *The Ministry of Healing*, p. 267.

59 Ibid.

60 White, *The Ministry of Healing*, p. 270.

61 *White, The Ministry of Healing, pp. 241-242.*

62 Abraham H. Maslow, 'A Theory of Human Motivation' in *Psychological Review 50*, no. 4, (1943), 370–396.

63 David Barlow and V. Mark Durand, *Abnormal Psychology: An Integrative Approach* (Stamford, CT: Cengage Learning, 7th edn, 2014),

64 Aaron Lazare, *On Apology* (NY: Oxford University Press, 204), p.24.

65 Jo-Ann Tsang; Michael E McCullough; Frank D Fincham, 'The Longitudinal Association Between Forgiveness and Relationship Closeness', *Journal of Social and Clinical Psychology 25*, no. 4, (2006), 448-472 (466); Geneviève Parent, 'Identifying Factors Promoting or Obstructing Healing and Reconciliation: Observations from an Exploratory Research field in ex-Yugoslavia', *International Journal of Peace Studies* 17, no. 1, (2012), 25-45 (26).

66 Ellen G White, *Patriarchs and Prophets* (Mountain View, CA: Pacific Press Publishing Association, 1890), pp. 210-211.

67 See Genesis 37:3, 4 for a repetitive use of 'love' and in verses 4, 5, 8 and 11 for the use of 'hatred/envy'.

68 The repetitive occurrence of the 'crying' motif is seen in Genesis 42:24; 43:31.

⁶⁹ Bill T. Arnold, *Genesis* (NY: Cambridge University Press, 2009), p.354

⁷⁰ Claus Westermann, *Joseph: Studies of the Joseph Stories in Genesis* (MN: Augsburg Fortress, 1996), p. 68.

⁷¹ The Holy Scripture recounts that "the Lord was with Joseph and he was a successful man; and he was in the house of his master the Egyptian. And his master saw that the Lord was with him and that the Lord made all he did to prosper in his hands." See Genesis 39: 2-4, 21-23.

⁷² Clare Amos, *The Book of Genesis* (Peterborough, UK: Epworth Press, 2004), p. 251.

⁷³ Westermann, *Joseph,* p. 79.

⁷⁴ The appearance of the 'weeping' motif is also seen in Genesis 45:2, 14.

⁷⁵ See Genesis 45:5-8; 50:20 for the main character's perspective of his sufferings.

⁷⁶ Arnold, *Genesis*, p.357.

⁷⁷ Amos, *The Book of Genesis*, p. 258.

⁷⁸ Westermann, *Joseph,* p. 96.

⁷⁹ White, *Patriarchs and Prophets*, p. 239.

⁸⁰ Arnold, *Genesis*, p. 387.

⁸¹ Joseph was thirty years when he came into the presence of Pharaoh to be selected as Governor of Egypt. See Genesis 41:46. He subsequently died at age 110 as recorded in Genesis 50:26.

⁸² See 1 John 4:7-19 for a theological perspective of the love-fear tension. Italics provided to this New Living Translation version of the text.

⁸³ See Genesis 50:21 in the Amplified Bible version.

⁸⁴ This biblical text is located in Jeremiah 17:9-10.

⁸⁵ Joseph had indicated his intentions to look after his brothers earlier in Genesis 45:11; 47:12.

⁸⁶ Genesis 50:21c reminds us that Joseph "comforted them *[his brothers]* and spoke kindly to them *[his brothers]*." Italics Added.

⁸⁷ "Love must be sincere. Hate what is evil; cling to what is good. Be devoted to one another in love. Honor one another above yourselves. Never be lacking in zeal, but

keep your spiritual fervor, serving the Lord. Be joyful in hope, patient in affliction, faithful in prayer" (Romans 12:9-12, NIV).

88 "But the fruit of the Spirit is love, joy, peace, forbearance, kindness, goodness, faithfulness, gentleness and self-control" (Galatians 5:22-23, NIV).

89 "Bless those who persecute you [who are cruel in their attitude toward you]; bless and do not curse them. Rejoice with those who rejoice [sharing others' joy], and weep with those who weep [sharing others' grief]. Live in harmony with one another; do not be haughty (snobbish, high-minded, exclusive), but readily adjust yourself to [people, things] *and* give yourselves to humble tasks. Never overestimate yourself *or* be wise in your own conceits. Repay no one evil for evil, but take thought for what is honest *and* proper *and* noble [aiming to be above reproach] in the sight of everyone" (Romans 12:14-17, AMP).

90 E G White, *Education*, 16-18.

91 See Genesis 37:18-20 for the narrative relating to this issue.

92 The occasions on which the brothers bowed down to Joseph are narrated in Genesis 42:6; 43:26; 44:14; and 50:18.

93 White, *Patriarchs and Prophets*, p. 216 – 217.

94 In White, *Patriarchs and Prophets*, p. 217, Joseph's ordeal with Potiphar's is given an insightful explanation.

95 White, *Patriarchs and Prophets*, p. 218.

96 White, *Patriarchs and Prophets*, pp. 217- 218.

97 White, *Patriarchs and Prophets*, p. 210.

98 White, *Patriarchs and Prophets*, p. 217.

99 White, *Patriarchs and Prophets*, p. 218.

100 Jon R. Webb, Loren Toussaint, Claire Z. Kalpakjian, and Denise G. Tate. 'Forgiveness and Health-related Outcomes among People with Spinal Cord Injury.' *Disability & Rehabilitation* 32, no. 5 (2010), 360-366 (361)

101 See E G White, *Desire of Ages, p. 83* for a discussion of the importance of reflecting on Christ's life.

[102] Witvliet van Oyen, Charlotte, Thomas E. Ludwig, and Kelly L. Vander Laan. 'Granting Forgiveness or Harboring Grudges: Implications for Emotion, Physiology, and Health.' *Psychological Science* 12, no. 2 (2001), 117-123.

[103] Webb, Toussaint, et al., 'Forgiveness and Health-related Outcomes among People with Spinal Cord Injury', 361.

ABOUT THE AUTHOR

Victor D. Marshall has a keen passion for the ministry of intercessory prayer, emotional health, and spirituality—which are powerful pathways to deepening one's relationship with God. He has also designed and set up the ten-week Relationship Restoration Programme aimed at assisting emotionally, and spiritually, unwell congregations, groups, and individuals in experiencing emotional wholeness. Furthermore, he organizes a series of emotional health seminars entitled A Balm in Gilead in his congregations on a yearly basis. Moreover, he is trained in special needs education, educational psychology, possesses an MA in pastoral studies, and works for the North England Conference of Seventh-day Adventists in the United Kingdom. With his dear wife, Maria, and son, Josiah, at his side, he presently pastors Doncaster, Sheffield Carterknowle and Sheffield Manor Seventh-day Adventist Churches in South Yorkshire, England.

A JOURNEY OF
THE BOLD AND
THE YOUNG:
LIVING ON THE EDGE

VICTOR D MARSHALL

VICTOR D. MARSHALL

SET THE CAPTIVES

Free

Experiencing Healing Through
Holistic Restoration

VICTOR D. MARSHALL

SET THE CAPTIVES

Free

workbook

12 Studies for Groups or Individuals

Printed in the United States
By Bookmasters